Student Workbook for

Public Relations Writing

Second Edition

Principles in Practice

Donald Treadwell
Jill B. Treadwell

For information:

Sage Publications, Inc.
2455 Teller Road
Thousand Oaks, California 91320
E-mail: order@sagepub.com

Sage Publications Ltd.
1 Oliver's Yard
55 City Road
London, EC1Y 1SP
United Kingdom

Sage Publications India Pvt. Ltd.
B-42 Panchsheel Enclave
Post Box 4109
New Delhi 110-017 India

05 06 07 08 09 10 9 8 7 6 5 4 3 2 1

Part One – Introduction and Employer Profiles

Part Two – Exercises

Chapter 16: High Profile Projects: Annual Reports, Events, and Expositions

Public Relations Writing
Principles in Practice

Introduction to the Workbook

During this course we suggest that you work for one client, for which you will produce most of your writing projects. This is a real-world situation – even if you work in an agency. It allows you to progressively make more sophisticated decisions based on what you have learned about your client and its environment. Perhaps as important, it encourages you to look at documents you have written previously and determine how you can adapt these documents to new audiences, new situations, or new media.

This workbook presents four clients that are simulations of actual organizations, but you can easily do all of the exercises and assignments using other simulated clients or even real-world clients as your professor determines.

Part One: Clients

Part One of this workbook introduces four simulated clients. They are:

- Central College – a private four-year college
- CommunicAID – a non-profit social services organization working with the homeless
- HealthWay Pharmacies, Inc. – a chain of retail pharmacies and mail-order service
- ValleyLINK Communications, an Internet service provider.

For each of the clients we present an introduction, an organizational history, a brief synopsis of the industry and its challenges, an organizational chart, a list of recent media releases, and basic financial information. The clients have been chosen to provide topical relevance, to represent public relations growth industries and both profit and non-profit organizations and to give you an idea of the breadth of organizations that employ public relations writers.

The clients are equal with regard to the amount and depth of background information provided. However, each of them has its own organizational culture that is reflected in the design and formatting of the client pages and in the background text itself. Understanding these differences will help you not only to select a client with which you are comfortable but also to write and design documents that will be appropriate for that client

Fill in the Blanks ...

IMPORTANT: We suggest that you define a real region within which your client will operate and that you substitute real cities, towns and states for the locations "Anytown, Othertown, YourState," etc. For example, you may choose to work in the region surrounding your campus. It should be large enough to have multiple publics, multiple media sources, but probably some natural boundaries, such as a valley, or half of your state, or a metropolitan area (including suburbs).

We have also left blank many names for you to complete.

Although it may be tempting to work for a national client, doing so will make it more difficult to identify and understand the publics you will be writing for and the available media you will use to reach them.

For each client we have provided several pages of introduction, about the client, its services, people, history, finances and policies. This is followed by special scenarios and information that applies to one or more of the writing assignments in Part Two.

"Getting Started"

At the end of Part One is a "Getting Started" section in which you will define the basic publics and media on which you will base your writing and writing decisions. Because familiarity with both will allow you to focus on real writing decisions, we have not defined the city or area in which any of the clients operate. Instead, we have defined them as working in Anytown, YourState (Anytown, YS). Instead, you will develop the profile from what you already know about your local area, from area guides and directories and from the websites for local towns and organizations.

Part Two: Exercises and Writing Assignments

Part Two includes all of the writing exercises. They provide practice in writing the documents discussed in the text. Moreover, they guide you through the thought processes and planning that will help you gather material and make decisions about the writing projects.

What you write and how you write it will depend on how your class is organized. Because they are grounded in real-world practices, few of the writing assignments have only a single answer. Answers will differ based on decisions you make about your audience, available media and the purpose of the communication. You should be able to defend and discuss any writing decisions you make. Whatever your specific writing assignments and however they are written, there will be no debate on the hallmarks of a successful public relations writer. In all cases your writing should be accurate, on time, and free of errors.

We hope the workbook and textbook will give you a sense of what public relations writing is all about and enthuse you to consider a career in public relations.

"Plan of Attack" forms

At the end of Part Two are the Plan of Attack forms referred to throughout the exercises. There is one for each major writing project plus some extras for additional assignments. The forms are perforated so that you can submit them to your professor if required. The forms guide you through the macro- and micro-level thinking you should be doing before writing each assignment. The first page of each form includes macro-level questions about audience, media, message and style that underpin all writing projects. The second page of each includes micro-level questions and exercises related to the specific project. In most cases, the forms also include a brief "Self-evaluation" in which you will examine and critique your own writing. This is always a good idea.

Dear Colleague:

It is my pleasure to welcome you as a member of the staff of Central College. At Central College our faculty, staff and administrators work as a team to provide the best educational experience possible for all our students. We work hard to fulfill the college mission and we are pleased to have you join us.

Two years ago we reviewed our position in the educational community and the needs of our constituent audiences to come up with a set of goals that we hope will secure our place as an educational leader well into the 21st century. Every position at the college has a place in this plan and yours is no exception. We look forward to your contributions.

The following manual explains much of what you need to know about our campus. Your supervisor or department head will personally explain your department and the particulars of your job. The manual also includes a copy of your contract and the rights and responsibilities of your job.

I believe that CC students are among the best in the country and that it is our duty to both challenge and encourage them. I invite your suggestions as to how we can improve the delivery of education to our current students and how we can broaden our base to include the wider Central College community.

I look forward to meeting all new staff as soon as possible. Please don't hesitate to introduce yourself whenever you see me on campus. In the meantime, welcome to our community.

Sincerely,

Leon C. DeWitt, Ph.D.
President

100 College Avenue, Anytown, YS 11111
Telephone: ZZZ-ZZZ-ZZZZ   Fax: ZZZ-ZZZ-ZZZY
www.centralcollege.edu

COLLEGE
ANNUAL GOALS

- Increase total enrollment 5 percent.

- Increase enrollment from outside YourState by 10 percent.

- Increase annual giving by 15 percent.

- Increase alumni participation by 20 percent, targeting new graduates and the 5-year anniversary classes.

- Increase business and community giving by 10 percent.

- Create and promote scholarship program for local students.

- Expand on-line satellite programs to remote sites in two neighboring towns.

- Open additional annex campus with satellite programs in Fartown, YS.

- Increase community participation in continuing education programs by offering advanced programs in Internet literacy and marketing by computer.

SAMPLE MEDIA
RELEASES
ISSUED IN THE
LAST CALENDAR
YEAR

NASA Legacy at CC: Science Communication Students Learn to Analyze and Communicate Pathfinder Data

CC Faculty Promotions Announced at Convocation

CC Enrollments Rise in Response to New Programs

Twelve CC Seniors Named to Who's Who in American College and Universities

Making the Most of Opportunities: Disabled Senior Named Most Active Student at CC

Local Lawyer Elected President of CC Alumni Association

No More Maligning College Food: CC Students Lick Their Lips at New Choices: Some of Them Even "Eat Healthy"

CC Sponsors On-Line Financial Aid Seminar for High School Seniors

CC Celebrates Long Serving Employees: 14 staff and faculty honored

CC *Commentator* wins National Journalism Award

"Look Out World; Here We Come!" Many CC Seniors Start Their Careers as Interns

Senator to speak at CC commencement

Senator welcomes 1,203 CC graduates into the "real world"

(Name of city) student graduates from Central College *(Sent to the hometown papers of all graduating students, individualized to the student)*

Alumna Bequest Puts CC Library On-Line

Literacy Tutoring, Storm Clean-up and PSA filming: CC Students Find Community Service Activities Rewarding.

COLLEGE INFORMATION

CC ADDRESSES

Main Campus — 100 College Avenue, Anytown, YS
Othertown Annex — 30 State Street, Othertown, YS

CAMPUS FACTS AND FACILITIES

CC Wellness Center — managed jointly by the college health services and athletic departments and located on the CC campus. It is open to the entire college community. It offers a range of fitness programs and equipment, including free-weights, Nautilus, high and low-impact aerobics and swimming as well as nutrition and health advice and counselling.

ALUMNI ASSOCIATION

Current Officers: President: Peter Smith, *(Development Dir. CommunicAID)*
First Vice Pres.: Sara L. McLean, *(Sales Dir. HealthWay)*
2nd Vice Pres.: Angie Mercer, *(Human Res. Mgr., ValleyLINK)*

CAMPUS MEDIA

Campus Update . . . *A* monthly campus-wide newsletter produced by the Public Affairs Office. Distributed in boxes located in all campus buildings, including dorms.

AlumNotes . . . . Magazine produced and mailed quarterly to all alumni.

CC Commentator . . . The student association newspaper published weekly during normal semesters. Distributed in boxes in the library, student center, commuter lounge, dining halls and dormitories

WCCR . . . . Campus-based cable TV station broadcasting M-F between 7 and 11 p.m. to all campus dormitory rooms and to Othertown residents whose cable subscription includes local access Channel 23.

WCCT . . . . Campus-based FM radio station operating daily between 5 pm and midnight on broadcast band 106.2

Electronic: . . . . Students have computer accounts through which they can send and receive e-mail and access college web sites.

STUDENT ACTIVITIES

Athletics — *Department Contact and Sports Information:* Alumni Fieldhouse. CC is a member of the YourState independent college athletic conference, fielding men's teams in football, soccer, basketball, baseball, golf, tennis, swimming, cross country and track, and women's teams in soccer, basketball, softball, tennis, cross country, track, gymnastics, golf and swimming, all at the IAAA level. Over 60 percent of the student body participates in one or more of our intramural programs.

Community Service Program — *Contact: Director of Community Studies.*
All CC students are required to participate in a minimum of 12 credit hours of approved community service activities prior to graduation. Projects approved for this program are listed monthly in the *CC Commentator* and on the bulletin board in the Community Studies Office. Approval may also be given on an individual basis for projects proposed by students. All projects must be undertaken in a 50-mile radius of Yourcity, YS.

Central College is a private, non-denominational, liberal arts college founded in 1902 to provide quality higher education to the citizens of Anytown, YourState. Today CC enrolls over 4,500 full-time students at our main campus in Anytown and an additional 825 at our campus annex in Othertown. Over 1,200 students also participate annually in our part-time, evening and weekend-seminar programs. Over 75 percent of our students live within a 150-mile radius of the college; 40 percent reside in Anytown itself. Sixty percent live on campus.

EDUCATIONAL PROGRAMS AND FACILITIES

Central College was the first institution of higher education in Anytown. Thirty-five students enrolled in its first term, all of them in education. By 1915 we had added majors in English and mathematics. Our first science lab opened in 1935; today our science programs in plant biology, anatomy, and applied chemistry are housed in the $8 million Miller-Johnson Science Center which opened in 1995.

Responding to the needs of WWII veterans who applied under the GI Bill, CC offered the valley's first courses in business administration and marketing. These programs are now combined in the Adams School of Business Management which has graduated many of the city's most prominent business and civic leaders.

Under a grant from the YourState Department of Educational Resources and a consortium of in-state software designers, CC launched the first college computer program in the valley in 1979. Originally the basis for a state-sponsored program to train local teachers in computers in the classroom, the lab is now the center of on-line technology in the valley, including both PC and Macintosh training as well as programs in software development and systems design.

CAMPUS GROWTH

The first president of Central College was retired Congressman Wilfred C. Kenwood, who donated the land for the first campus and led a campaign among Central Valley residents to fund construction of the first dormitory. Kenwood Hall, home of the Alumni Office, is the original estate of Congressman Kenwood. Additional property has been acquired by donation, purchase from the Auburn City Council and through a 200-acre trade with the Anycity Power Authority.

The Alumni Property Endowment, begun in 1952 to mark the college's 50th anniversary, provides funding for campus and building maintenance and makes it possible for CC to consistently rank among the most beautiful campuses in the region.

ANNEX CAMPUSES

In 1990, CC opened an annex campus in Othertown to service the particular needs of central YourState residents. For example, the Othertown campus offers full-time day-care at a site adjacent to the campus and there is an emphasis on after-hours degrees. Through a sophisticated on-line network annex students participate in classes at the Othertown campus and work interactively with professors at the Anytown campus. This program has been the model for similar experiments in on-line education throughout the state.

BOARD OF TRUSTEES
|
PRESIDENT ——— **Legal Counsel**
Leon C. DeWitt, Ph.D

Vice President, Administration/Fiscal Affairs: John D. Clauson, CPA, JD
    Director of Human Resources — Susan Anderson
    Director of Administration
        Manager of Accounting
        Bookstore Manager
        Food Service Manager
    Director of Physical Plant
    Director of Administrative Computing
    Bursar

Vice President, Academic Affairs: Mary C. O'Neil, Ph.D.
    Dean of Undergraduate Studies
    Dean of Graduate Studies
    Dean of Faculty
    Director of the Library
    Director of Academic Computing — Antoine St. Pierre
    Director of Admissions
    Director of Financial Aid
    Registrar — James Spencer

Vice President, Student Affairs: Frank Winter, Ph.D.
    Director of Housing
    Director of Student Activities
    Director of Religious and Counselling Services
    Director of Health Services
    Director of Athletics

Vice President, College Relations: Kristopher Kaman
    Director of Development - Jack Marshall
    Director of Alumni Affairs - Maria Suarez
    Director of Public Affairs - Alison Jones
        News Bureau
        Public Relations
        Community Relations
        Sports Information
    Director of Marketing

Vice President, Special Programs: Katherine Wang, Ph.D.
    Director of Community Studies
    Director of Satellite Campus Development
    Director of Summer Programs
    Director of Conference Services

FINANCIAL INFORMATION AND GROWTH STATISTICS

	This Year	Last Year
INCOME		
Student tuition and fees	$ 33,500,000	$ 31,000,000
Fundraising		
Alumni	325,000	270,000
Corporations and foundations	75,000	50,000
Other fundraising	25,000	20,000
Other	1,500,000	1,000,000
Total Income	$35,425,000	$ 32,340,000
EXPENSES		
Instruction (salaries, insurance)	$14,250,000	$14,000,000
Administration	6,000,000	5,750,000
Facilities (rent, insurance)	3,900,000	3,400,000
Athletic Department	3,400,000	2,900,000
Advertising and promotion	500,000	450,000
Interest on long-term debt	300,000	375,000
Auxiliary expenses	6,250,000	5,500,000
Total expenses	34,600,000	32,375,000
NET Income (Loss)	**$ 825,000**	**($35,000)**

Annual Fund Growth		Growth in Student Numbers	
		Full time	Part time
6 years ago $243,000		4,400	750
5 years ago $260,000		4,500	800
4 years ago $295,000		4,700	900
3 years ago $282,000		4,800	1,000
2 years ago $310,000		5,100	1,000
Last year $350,000		5,000	1,100
This year $425,000		5,385	1,200

Web sites: *To get you started:*

ScholarStuff Web page: www.scholarstuff.com

You can search by state for colleges/universities. There is also some financial aid, testing and job search info that you might find useful.

DEFINITION
Administrative staff are defined as all personnel employed by the following departments: President's Office, Academic Affairs, Student Affairs, College Relations, Admissions, Financial Aid, Alumni, Financial Services (including Bursar) and the technical/secretarial support staff for academic departments.

OFFICE HOURS
All administrative offices of Central College are open Monday - Friday from 8 am to 5 pm. Summer hours are 7 am to 4 pm. The Admissions Office and Financial Aid Offices are also open by appointment between 8 am and noon on Saturdays from October through May.

All administrative employees are employed to work a 40-hour week. You may be required to work outside the normal office hours, such as to staff an Alumni Weekend. If so, you may claim an equal amount of compensatory time within the month following the event. You must obtain the approval of your supervisor prior to taking the compensatory time.

Lunch hour for administrative staff is from 12:30 to 1:30. Offices will be open during this time to accommodate students and visitors. Department managers are responsible for ensuring that sufficient staff are on duty to handle the expected traffic and it is expected that all staff will participate in this duty by rotation.

PERSONAL SPACE
The offices of administrative staff are public areas and they present the public with an image of the college. The CC Art Department has put together a collection of posters, paintings, photographs and student artwork that may be loaned to employees for their offices. This selection represents traditional to modern art and offers pieces that should appeal to all staff. Administrative employees may not hang any artwork except from this selection. To view the selection, please contact the receptionist at the Phillips Art Gallery in Logan Hall. The Maintenance Department should be contacted to hang the selected pieces.

You may bring personal photos and small mementos for your desk, however, CC is not responsible for the safety or security of any personal objects you bring to the office.

BREAK ROOMS
Administrative staff may eat in the dining commons or campus snack and juice bars for lunch and breaks. There is also a central campus "Staff Room" located in Bates Hall. It has sofas and a television set as well as a microwave oven and refrigerator. This room is cleaned nightly. The refrigerator is cleaned each weekend and all food left there over the weekend will also be disposed of unless clearly marked.

Many individual departments and offices also have coffee, tea and hot chocolate mix for their staff. Each of these "coffee clubs" have their own rules of organization and are not the responsibility of the college. The college requires that coffee pots and microwaves are kept out of public areas where visitors could see them. The equipment must be checked by the Maintenance Department before installation to ensure that it complies with campus fire codes.

BACKGROUND TO WRITING ASSIGNMENTS – CENTRAL COLLEGE

Following is background information you will need for some of the writing exercises in this workbook. Instructions for the exercises can be found in Part Two of the workbook.

ORGANIZATIONAL CULTURE

BACKGROUND TO EXERCISE 4-2

The Central College Director of Human Resources has received the following memo from college president, Dr. DeWitt.

President's Office

Memo to: Susan Anderson
              Director of Human Resources
From: Leon DeWitt
              President
Re: Dress standards for administrative staff

Susan:

I was walking around campus yesterday afternoon and stopped in the bursar's office to see Jim Spencer. There were several groups of people and I couldn't decide which ones were students and which were staff. I wanted to see if Jim was in and I didn't know whom to ask.

I think it's time we instituted some level of dress policy for administrative staff so that we present a more professional image. I know we can't do anything about the faculty because their union would scream "academic freedom," and the maintenance and food services people already have their own dress requirements. Besides they aren't the ones to give me the problem; and for the most part they aren't in the public eye either.

I think "corporate casual" is the word the business community uses to describe what I have in mind. No t-shirts or jeans or other clothes that look like they belong on a playing field. And be sure you make it clear that the policy includes student workers in the administrative departments. It won't hurt them to understand that the "real world" has standards. Let's avoid issues like skirt lengths and necklines unless you think it's really necessary. VPs and department heads also need to know that for special functions coats and ties or dresses and heels or whatever — you know what I mean — are still a must.

Please think this through and give me a draft by next week. You probably have some samples in your files to help. I don't want this to be onerous, but I don't think we're sending an appropriate message about our college, and we've got the accreditation committee coming through in a few months.

Thanks for your help with this. I look forward to seeing what you come up with.

NEWS WRITING

BACKGROUND TO EXERCISE 9-4

Good News! The president of Central College has just received the following notice from the director of the YourState Educational Research Foundation (YSERF).

YourState Educational Research Foundation
Foundation Place, Addison YS 01234

Dr. Leon C. DeWitt
President
Central College
100 College Avenue
Anytown, YS 11111

Dear Dr. DeWitt:

Congratulations! The YourState Research Foundation (YSERF) is pleased to notify you that Central College is one of five institutions of higher education selected to participate in "Early Support", a four-year pilot study of long-distance remedial education funded jointly by the YSERF and the YourState Department of Education. The other institutions are: *(you may name).*

These institutions have been selected because of their demonstrated capabilities in electronic learning and expertise in one or more subject areas to be included in the program. Although final designation of the subject matter programs to be developed by Central College is pending, it is expected that you will be responsible for programs in computer skill development and basic English, including writing.

The first meeting of the college and university participants will take place at the Capitol on the fifteenth of this month. At that time we will discuss the high schools with which each college will be partnered and the basic course curriculum to be developed.   At a minimum, please send to the meeting your institutional project director and at least one of the participating professors or program developers. Further details will be sent directly to these people.

Ms. Joanne Robinson, education officer, has been assigned as foundation liaison for this project. If you require any assistance from our office, please contact her directly at (200) 929-0744.

Sincerely,

J.D. Philips
Research Director

Continued....

WHAT DOES THIS MEAN TO CENTRAL COLLEGE?

The following information will help you determine what public relations strategy, if any, should be pursued as the result of this announcement.

1.   PROGRAM DETAILS: The five participating colleges/universities will be linked with each other and with a network of high schools in their region. Together they will develop remedial education programs to bring high school juniors and seniors deemed to be academically marginal up to college level in reading, writing, math and computer skills *before* they enter college. It is expected that helping these students begin college at the same level as, rather than behind their peers, will markedly improve the graduation rate of these students.

The students will be identified by a joint team of high school and college counselors and foundation analysts at the end of their sophomore year in high school and will participate exclusively in the on-line program for the final two years of high school. Courses will be developed and taught on-line by college personnel. Their progress will also be monitored and reported at the high school level.

Students will attend classes at interactive classrooms set up throughout YourState. All equipment for these classrooms will be provided under a grant from the Federal Educational Resources Commission.

CC has agreed to accept for admission, and to provide financial aid to all applicants from the participating high schools who perform satisfactorily in the program.

An oversight panel from the YSERF will monitor the program and allocate funds to participating institutions.

2.   CC RESPONSIBILITIES: The CC proposal commits you to appointing the Director of Academic Computing, as full-time director of the grant project. The college also committed to appointing a team of five support staff, including three program developers/professors to the program. All of these personnel will be supported by the grant.

3.   OTHER RELEVANT INFORMATION: The CC Board of Trustees has approved a directive to the Admissions Department to raise the admission standards of incoming freshmen over the next five years. This would make CC more competitive with "Ivy-League" caliber institutions.

The effect of this test program on the GPA/SAT/ACT scores of entering students, and on the overall admissions level of the College will not be known until the end of the study and the college is committed to accepting all students who pass the course.

4.   SCHEDULE: Central College will execute the program by working with the following schools: *(you may name).*

FEATURE WRITING

BACKGROUND TO EXERCISE 10-2

The following information is the raw material for a feature story that the Central College Development Office wants to use in its annual report to annual fund contributors who are primarily alumni but also include parents, friends and faculty. The Director of Development believes this article will add some "human interest" to the report.

The basis of the story is the "Early Support" pilot program, the long-distance remedial education program in which CC is one of five participating institutions named to participate and on which you previously wrote a news release. The information below should give you a wide range of options for writing this story.

PROGRAM DATA AND STATISTICS

- The program began with the following courses offered. Faculty for the courses were selected from the five participating colleges. The curriculum and course content were decided jointly by the teaching faculty and high school representatives.

- Classes were "taught" by participating faculty using the interactive classroom at each college, with the class transmitted to the interactive classrooms at the participating high schools. Professors and students were required to communicate regularly on-line.

- To manage the program, the participating colleges also worked with local schools to resolve computer issues and evaluate the program.

- CC personnel taught classes using the interactive classroom facilities at the anytown campus.

  CC was responsible for teaching writing and computer skills courses. Teaching faculty were provided by the English, Communication and Computer Departments.

- Faculty and academic counselors at the participating high schools nominated a total of 100 high school seniors who they believed would benefit from the program. English is the second language for approximately 25% of the students.

  The selected students had placed below average on a sample SAT test but were believed by faculty to be able to benefit from remedial programs in writing, history and computing as well as individualized attention in other subjects.

- Results: end of year 1

  The average SAT scores of students in the program increased by 200 points over their previous score. The greatest increases were in reading comprehension and writing skills, but this is believed to also be the basis for increase in other areas.

  This was sufficient to allow 85 of the seniors in the program to be accepted by an institution participating in the program. Five others opted to remain in high school and spend another year in the program in order to improve their scores and abilities more. The rest did not increase their SAT scores and were not accepted by the participating institutions under the terms of the original agreement between the students and institutions. An abnormally high number of absences were blamed for the problems experienced by these students.

Spokespersons

The following people could be expected to be the subject of this article and/or would comment for this article, depending on the topic and theme you choose to pursue. It is your responsibility to select the appropriate spokespersons and to write any quotes from them. Next to each person we have identified the attitude this person would likely have toward the project. This attitude should be reflected in his or her words.

Except for the CC personnel and the mayor (whom you have previously identified), you may name any of the people. You may assume that anyone in an official capacity has agreed that his or her name may be used, but it is possible some of the private citizens may not wish to be named. How can you deal with this?

Possible spokesperson	Attitude/message
* Central College president	Positive; credit staff, city, community; aware of public relations opportunity, mission-driven
* Early Support program director	Positive; credit staff
* Anytown Mayor	Enthusiastic; political; take some credit
* Heads of affiliated high schools	Positive; appreciative, forward-looking
* Faculty that participated in the program	Positive; focused on students
* Students who participated in the program	Enthusiastic; positive; inspired
* Representative of YSERF	Positive, political, forward-looking

NEWSLETTERS

BACKGROUND TO EXERCISES 10-4 AND 10-5

You are responsible for compiling the monthly campus newsletter and quarterly alumni newsletter.   In each case it is the first issue after the new calendar year. The following stories are the raw material for both newsletters.

Completing the exercise in the text for this assignment will help you determine which articles to include in each document. Be aware that these items are presented "as you received them." They are not necessarily grammatical or consistent in style. That is your job.

- Dress code announcement: It has been approved as you wrote it. The HR Director wants to see a draft of the article for the newsletter as soon as possible. *(Note: She is concerned staff will react badly to this perceived threat because it is not also aimed at faculty and students). HINT: What tone should you take? Why? Can you think of another way to handle the subject?*

- Alumni Association President's Message: He wants suggestions on a topic for this month.

- CC selected for "Early Support" program: The news story you wrote in Exercise 9-4 will be the basis for the lead news story for the newsletters. Exercise 10-5 will guide you through adapting this story to newsletter style.

- News sent in from annex campuses: *Note: You will get this type of information from depart-ment/annex correspondents, even chairs and directors. What to use is always a tough decision without hurting anyone's feelings or discouraging future contributions.*

  - Othertown staff celebrated the first anniversary of opening of their campus center with morning doughnuts provided by receptionist _____ and an after-work party at the Mountain View Restaurant. Thanks to Dr. DeWitt for joining us and for his kind words of congratulations.

- Births: *Following are notices you saw on the bulletin board in the staff room in Alumni Hall:* "Maintenance supervisor _____ is passing out pink cigars; His girlfriend _____ had a baby girl." "Football trainer _____ and his wife ____ new baby is a real bruiser, just like his Dad. 9 lbs. 4 oz."

- Engagements: *Following is a phone message from "Sandy" in Othertown. "_____ got engaged. The ring is huge! Can it go in the newsletter?"*

- Accounting News: W-2 tax forms will be out to all employees by the end of the month. If you have any questions refer them to the business office, Extension 447.

- Weddings: *(You may name)*

- Long Service: *Following is a memo from the HR Vice President. "The following staff and faculty have received long service awards Please feature in next newsletter."*

Fifteen years:	_____, Assoc. Prof., Communications
Ten years:	_____, Trainer, Athletic Department
	_____, Mail clerk
Five years:	_____, Dept. Sec., English
	_____, Accounting
	_____, Asst. Prof., History

- Faculty Notes:

  The annual commencement art show will be works by _____, prof/art. He does mixed media work, usually acrylics and natural fibers. The theme of the show will be "CC: one man's Vision of the future".

  _____, assoc. prof/history, published article in *Historical Monographs*, Fall edition. Article titled "Internet Resources for Historical Research: Treasures Uncovered".

- Sports Notes: *(You can decide as appropriate to your audience and the season)*

- Illness: _____'s father is recovering from surgery. _____'s son, _____, broke his leg.

- Suggestions: The following were found in the Suggestion Box during the last month.

  "I think we should have a special recognition for the Employee of the Month in each office. How about reserving the parking spot closest to the door for that person."

  "The cleaning lady should wash the dishes if they are left in the sink."

- Alumni Calendar: *(You may decide)*

- New Employees: _____ – Admin. ass't, Alumni Office. She will be responsible for updating alumni files and compiling the Class Notes section of the alumni newsletter.

  _____ – Purchasing. She has replaced Joan Talbot who transferred to the bookstore. Sondra is the new contact for supplies.

  _____ – Assistant professor, business management

- Newsletter Staff:
  Editor - You
  Others: *(You may name)*
  Student intern: _____ *(public relations major)*

- Alumni Newsletter:
  Editor: You
  Board: Maria Suarez, *Alumni Director*
  Allison Jones, *Director of Public Affairs*
  _____, *Alumni Fund*
  Class Notes: _____

- Cartoon: *Note scrawled on a fax from the Bursar. "Found this cartoon in my file the other day. Hope it is clear enough for you to use."*

- Admissions Update The Admissions Department wants to thank alumna _____ *(include graduation year)* for hosting an open admissions forum at their home in Othertown on December 28th with high school seniors, CC students and some faculty. This is a new admissions thrust.

CRISIS WRITING

BACKGROUND TO EXERCISES 12-1 AND 12-2

Sometimes it is necessary to publicly address issues that may embarrass or otherwise show your employer in a "less than favorable" light. Many public companies have been faced with this situation when their administrators were charged with financial malfeasance, processes were shown to be environmentally irresponsible or promotions suspected of deliberately violating "truth in advertising" laws, for example. Following is a scenario in which you must publicly address a situation that has the potential to impact relationships with one or more of your organization's key publics.

Important Background Information:

Central College has always prided itself on the level of support it receives from its alumni, 75% of whom live in the greater Anytown community. Annual fund contributions have nearly doubled over the last three years as alumni and the community alike have responded to requests to "join a partnership for a better community." Alumni contributions are especially valuable as foundations look for evidence of support from within the organizational family as part of their funding criteria.

The Development Office (i.e., fundraising office) has put special effort into developing donor incentive programs and especially into cultivating alumni and several high-profile, wealthy citizens as the foundation for a scholarship campaign that the college plans to launch in three months. The goal of the capital campaign is to raise $15 million for the scholarship endowment. It will be the largest fundraising campaign ever undertaken by Central College

The Situation:

Two months ago, Central College development officer Albert Mathison was terminated for falsifying expense reports. Now, on the eve of the capital campaign, a disgruntled Mathison has written a letter to the editor of the Anytown daily newspaper. The letter charges the Central College administration with "extravagant expenditures" including luxury dinners and annual administrator "retreats" at five-star holiday resorts and that President DeWitt routinely takes his wife, at college expense to conferences. Mathison claims that these expenditures were made possible by diverting a percentage of the contributions made to the Annual Fund into the Central College president's "discretionary budget".

The newspaper editor has assigned a reporter to follow up on the charges and determine if they are true and if it is indeed, a story. The reporter intends to file the story with or without college comment. Your inquiries show that the story is indeed true. A percentage of the Annual Fund monies had been put under the control of the president's assistant. The account is being used to pay for the items Mathison mentioned. Ms. DeWitt, who holds a Ph.D. in English, pays her own way to conferences at which she is a participant.

Reaction: The Central College president's reaction is that all funds have been accounted for (which is true) and that he uses the account to effectively develop contacts who will contribute to future projects for the college. A case in point is the current capital campaign for which Central College has already secured $5 million in donations from a charitable foundation and two Anytown businessmen. The relationships on which these donations are made, he argues, cannot be developed by mail or over a cup of coffee. He also argues that part of the cultivation process often involves social occasions at which his wife's presence is appropriate.

Also, you know that the staff retreat in question was held at the lakeside estate of a board member who offers the facility to all of the charitable organizations she supports.

PERSUASIVE MESSAGES

BACKGROUND TO EXERCISES 14-3 AND 14-4

This background information will be used for three assignments in Chapter Fourteen. It is a scenario in which Central College might feel compelled to issue a persuasive message.

NOTE: CommunicAID, another of the text clients, will be writing in opposition to your message. For the "Letter to the Editor" assignment you should assume that the Anytown newspaper has printed an editorial supporting the retention of funds that pay for social services for the needy and homeless rather than funds for education.

The Situation

The economic crisis in YourState does not abate, and Governor _____ continues to make cuts in the grants to non-profit and educational institutions. Central College receives 40% of its funding through subsidies and grants from YourState government agencies. The most recent round of cuts reduced their administrative budgets by over $600,000, and rumors abound that more cuts will come. Word on the street is that the cuts will hit either higher education or social services for the needy and homeless.

These cuts have already impacted the staffing levels for several of the college's community initiatives and additional cuts will likely result in reduced hours for the public athletic facilities and library. The cuts have also affected the ability of Central College to increase fundraising activities in the private sector that would reduce the effect of the cuts to its programs.

You have been working with the team that is developing the organization's response to these cuts. Among other tactics, you have recommended to President DeWitt that the College should make a greater effort to persuade the Anytown legislative representatives to vote against any cuts to higher education and to carry your message to the governor and state legislature.

You have recommended a two-pronged strategy:

1.	Contacting the legislators directly; and
2.	Getting the community to add its voice to the cause.

The Central College president has directed you to draft the letter to the legislature and "letter to the editor" of the Anytown newspaper for this campaign.

Note: You are free to determine some details of the effects of the cuts, but do not assume that the college is in danger of closing based on current projections.

TRADE FAIRS AND CONFERENCES

BACKGROUND TO EXERCISE 16-8

Central College will participate in the educational recruitment fair sponsored by the YourState Association of Colleges and Universities (YSACU). Vendors typically include approximately 80 YS colleges and universities, 60 institutions from neighboring states plus 25 banks and other suppliers of services and equipment. The conference attracts over 2,500 high school juniors and seniors (and their families) plus 1,200 students currently enrolled in college.

Conference Details:	Date: ....Friday Oct. 2 (4-8 p.m.) and Saturday Oct. 3 (9 a.m. -8.p.m.) at the Colony Crest Hotel, Othertown, YS.

Theme: ......The theme for the conferences will be "Education for All"

<u>Display Details:</u>	Booths: ....8' x 8' spaces, Booth #34 at both conferences will be reserved as the YSACU information booth.
	Standard: ....Each booth will include one 3' x 6' table with gray skirt plus gray backdrop, three electric outlets.
	Extras: ....Television and video monitors, VCRs at additional cost.
	Food Service: ..Coffee, tea, soft drinks and sandwiches will be available at designated locations throughout the fair.
	Program: ....Conference organizers produce a program that includes a listing of the names and addresses of all vendors. They will also accept ads for this program.
<u>Vendor Schedule:</u>	The official drawing for any prizes offered by individual vendors will be held at the YSACU booth at 6 p.m. on Saturday evening.
<u>Media Coverage:</u>	Local press and TV stations are likely to attend both conferences for photo and story potential. In addition, the Anytown newspaper's annual educational supplement is published in August, two weeks before the Education Fair, and advertising space is available.
<u>CC Focus:</u>	Central College's purpose in attending this conference is to attract new students, both high school students and transfers from other colleges.

The focus will be on a new initiative called "Tradition and Technology", the college's mission for the early 21st century. Under this program, the college will explore how technology can be used to support traditional disciplines. The "Tradition and Technology" program will begin as part of a new bachelor's concentration in Educational Technology and expand into other departments over the next three years, ending with a campus in which technology is fully integrated into all other disciplines.

CC will use its participation in the "Early Support" program as evidence of its technological expertise, including the seven-minute video and brochure you have produced on the program.

CommunicAID

CARING FOR THE COMMUNITY

577 West Street, Anytown YS 00111
Phone: (XXX) 444-0000, Fax (XXX) 444-0001
www.communicaid.org

Dear Team Member:

Welcome to the CommunicAID family. You are about to join a dedicated team whose focus is on helping the poor and homeless in the greater Anytown community and we look forward to sharing our vision and our satisfying work with you.

First and foremost, CommunicAID is about people — both the members of our team and the people we serve. In our XX years of working with the Anytown community, we have achieved a reputation for caring, creativity and commitment, the three C's that underlie all our programs.

You have been selected to join our team because we believe you share our vision for a better Anytown and because you have demonstrated the creative communication abilities we seek in all our team members. We are a collaborative organization and we value new ideas and new approaches. We look forward to your input to our programs.

This team manual will introduce you to the CommunicAID organization as well as to the benefits to which you will be entitled. It sets out the guidelines by which we conduct our operations and the standards by which we conduct ourselves. You will find us to be an inclusive, equal-opportunity organization, so if you have any questions about the manual, the organization or your duties, do not hesitate to talk with your supervisor, the Human Resources staff or other colleagues on the CommunicAID team.

Again, welcome to CommunicAID. I hope you find your employment with us rewarding on a personal as well as professional level. Welcome to our team.

Sincerely,

Suzanne J. McGrath, MSW.
Director

Mission and Goals

CommunicAID Goals for current year

Communication: ....To ensure that all agencies with which we work have a communication plan for reaching the constituences that are in need of their services and that can provide necessary support.

....To develop a quarterly newsletter for the staffs of CommunicAID and its affiliated organizations.

....To develop a quarterly newsletter for Anytown residents.

Education: ....To increase exposure of all Anytown residents to the programs offered by CommunicAID and its affiliated agencies and organizations.

Funding: ....To secure increased funding for CommunicAID by 20% in the coming fiscal year. This money is used for CommunicAID salaries, rentals and all communication tasks.

....To assist all affiliated agencies to increase funding for their own services by 20% in the coming fiscal year. These funds go in full to support for the agency's programs.

Volunteer support ....To increase the level of volunteer support for CommunicAID by 10%. These volunteers provide counselling and paperwork assistance at the CommunicAID site.

....To assist all affiliate agencies and organizations to increase their volunteer support by 10% in the coming fiscal year.

Community Outreach:......To establish and staff additional CommunicAID centers in _____ and _____ . (Student to name appropriate locations).

....To establish summer activity programs for Elms Elementary students.

History

CommunicAID was founded in 1994 by a group of citizens who were concerned by the rising number of homeless in Anytown and by the apparent lack of services to assist them. What began as an effort to lobby the YourState government to fund a homeless shelter quickly turned into a full-fledged private community effort. The founding group was soon joined by the Anytown Council of Churches which had been running small food pantries from the basements of two of its member churches.

The original aim of the group (which called itself "The Poverty Program") was to care for the homeless by providing food and shelter. However, the mission quickly expanded to one of attacking the problem on a larger scale by helping the homeless find work and housing that would allow them to escape from their poverty status.

The first breakthrough was the donation of free office space at the Anytown Medical Center. This allowed CommunicAID (under its new name) to hire a full-time director. The Medical Center provided clerical support and communication services. The director's job was to research and create a profile of the Anytown homeless population. This profile is updated annually and serves as the basis for CommunicAID planning and services.

Because of the existing small food pantries, CommunicAID first focused on feeding the homeless. Within a year CommunicAID conducted its first fundraising campaign from which one of the food pantries was doubled in size and the other turned into a soup kitchen three days a week staffed by volunteers. These volunteers eventually formed "Food Banks United" as an affiliate of CommunicAID. This group is responsible for all food and nutrition programs under the CommunicAID umbrella.

In 1998 CommunicAID secured a grant from the YourState Housing Authority for the renovation of a building on West Street for the CommunicAID offices (the current premises) and the city's first homeless shelter. CommunicAID established an affiliation with Homes for All to develop housing services. Since 2001 the Anytown Literacy Coalition and Back-to-Work have also become affiliates.

CommunicAID itself has grown to include a Development Department to raise funds and IT and Communication Departments to provide computer, advertising and public relations services for both CommunicAID and the affiliates. The structure is designed to allow the affiliates to spend their time and funds developing and providing programs and services.

CommunicAID
CARING FOR THE COMMUNITY

Structure and Administration

Affliate organizations

Anytown Council of Churches

Anytown Regional Literacy Coalition
runs teen and adult literacy programs at
local libraries and homeless shelters
in the Anytown region.

Food Banks United
coordinates the activities of food banks
in the Anytown region

Homes for All
coordinates the activities of homeless
shelters and low income housing
developers in the Anytown region

Back-to-Work
provides assessment, job training,
counselling and placement services
in the Anytown region

Government Agencies

YourState Department of Health and
Human Services
YourState Department of Housing
Anytown Housing Authority
Anytown Transport Authority

Transportation Services
Anytown Regional Bus Services
Anytown Regional Cab Services

CommunicAID Board of Trustees

J.J. Barnes, Esq., *Community Rep.*
L.C. DeWitt, Pres., *Central College*
_____, *Anytown Mayor*
Rev. Paul Joseph, *Pres., Anytown Council of Churches*
Jon J. McLeod, *Pres., Anytown Medical Center*
Jane Monson, *Director, Anytown Literacy Coalition Affiliate rep.*
S.F. Petrocelli, MD, *Community Rep*
V.M. Singh, MD, *Community Rep.*
Alan.O. Smith, *YourState Housing Authority*
Jeff Marshall, *VP HealthWay Pharmacies*
Lynn Smith, *Dir., Administration, ValleyLINK.*

CommunicAID Adminstration

President
Suzanne. J. McGrath, MSW

General Counsel
E.W. Parsons

Director of Administration and Human Resources
Wang Lee

Director, Counselling Services
Andrea Jeffers

Director, Information Systems
James. S. Harmon

Director of Development
Peter Smith

Director of Communications and Media
Lori Smythe

Copy specialists
Elizabeth. E. Dorn
(Your name) _____

Grahic specialist
Claire Martin

CommunicAID
CARING FOR THE COMMUNITY

Media Releases and Web Sites

<u>Sample press releases issued during the last six months</u>

- $1 million grant launches $5 million CommunicAID capital campaign

- Housing specialist to Head CommunicAID service

- Weak Economy Puts New Pressures on Anytown Housing

- CommunicAID to Host Regional Seminar on Low Income Housing

- CommunicAID Staff Take the Lead During Poverty Awareness Week

- Anytown Restaurants Team to Support Regional Food Banks

- $25,000 Council of Churches Grant to Support Anytown Food Banks

- Downtown Food Pantry Joins CommunicAID agencies

- CommunicAID Staff Support United Way

- Auxiliary Holiday Fair Benefits CommunicAID programs

- CommunicAID Public Lecture Series to Focus on Integrated Housing for Seniors and Low Income Families.

- CommunicAID Fund Drive sets new record

<u>Web sites</u>

U.S. Department of Health and Human Services:..............www.hhs.gov

U.S. Department of Housing and Urban Development......www.hud.gov

Project Bread ....www.projectbread.org

ShareourStrength ....www.strength.org

Help the Homeless..www.helpthehomelessdo.org

National Center for Homeless Education ....www.serve.org/nche

Summer Food Service Program...www.usda.gov

CommunicAID
CARING FOR THE COMMUNITY

Financial Information and Growth Statistics

Income and Expenses
For CommunicAID and affiliates

	This Year	Last Year
REVENUE		
Grants	$ 1,150,000	$ 750,000
Restricted for building purchase	750,000	0
Subsidies from government agencies	3,500,000	5,100,000
Fundraising	3,450,000	1,500,000
Total Revenue	$ 8,850,000	$ 7,150,000
EXPENSES		
Personnel	3,700,000	3,500,000
Rent	400,000	400,000
Equipment and supplies	3,500,000	3,100,000
Building purchase	750,000	0
Interest on long-term debt	400,000	0
Total Expenses	$ 8,750,000	7,000,000
Net after expenses	**$ 100,000**	**$ 150,000**

Fundraising Growth Statistics
for CommunicAID and affiliates

	Annual Funds	Special Gifts*
Three years ago	$ 500,000	$ 100,000
Two years ago	$ 725,000	600,000
Last year	$ 950,000	1,000,000
This year	$1,200,000	$2,250,000

* Designated for specific projects, including property and equipment.

Policy Manual

Policies for CommunicAID Employees

Definition

CommunicAID employees are defined as all personnel employed on a full- or part-time basis to fill the following functions: administration, accounting, human resources, reception, clerical, counselling, and communications. This does not include persons working in a volunteer capacity or who are employed by CommunicAID affiliate organizations.

Hours of Employment

The CommunicAID center is open Monday-Friday 8 am - 8 pm, and Saturday 8 am - 3 pm. All staff work a five-day schedule to complement the activities of the center. At the time of your employment, you will be advised regarding the schedule for your position.

Department managers have the responsibility to ensure that their department is staffed to CommunicAID standards at all times.

Lunch hour is from 12:30 to 1:30, with the provision that at least one staff member must remain in each department during this time. Lunch hours for shift employees may be taken at any time with the approval of the department supervisor. Most departments have established lunch and break schedules.

Personal Space

All CommunicAID offices are considered public areas. Nothing personal may be hung on any walls. You may bring personal photos and small mementos for your desk, however CommunicAID is not responsible for the safety or security of any such objects.

Break Rooms

There is a cafe in the basement of the building next door and there are other small restaurants and take-away bars in the neighborhood Staff receive a 30 percent discount on all food and beverages purchased from the cafe. Show your staff ID card when paying the cashier. We expect to negotiate additional discounts with other facilities.

A "Staff Room" located behind the third floor conference room has staff lockers, sofas and both a men's and women's lounge. This area is restricted to CommunicAID staff. Staff may use any of the lockers; however, you are responsible for bringing your own lock. Employees are required to comply with any request by the Security Officers to open their lockers at any time.

Background to Writing Assignments: CommunicAID

Following is background information you will need for some of the writing exercises in this workbook. Instructions for the exercises can be found in Part Two of the workbook.

Organizational Culture

Background for Exercise 4-2

The CommunicAID Director of Human Resources recently received the following memo signed by the directors of development, accounting, and counselling. She confirmed the claims made in the memo and added some research regarding dress codes before referring the memo to the Director of Administration and Human Resources who agreed to submit it to the Board for approval.

Dear _____:

Until now, CommunicAID policy has been that employees must dress in what is considered "formal business" attire. This has been defined as coats and ties for men and dresses or suits and heels for women.

In light of the fact that all of our affiliate organizations including the government agencies have adopted more liberal dress code policies, we believe that CommunicAID should similarly relax our dress standards. In addition to improving the morale of our staff, particularly the younger members who see their peers in other industries dress more casually and who have more financial pressures in maintaining a formal work wardrobe, we believe this will also reap benefits in making our interactions with our homeless clients less intimidating. We believe what is known as "business casual" will be appropriate.

We recognize the possible concern that "relaxed" does not become sloppy or unprofessional and assure you that we will be happy to establish written limits on what is acceptable. We are committed to maintaining our high standards of professional conduct....even in a "relaxed" atmosphere.

If you would like the specifics of the attire we hope to adopt please do not hesitate to contact either of us. Thank you for your help with this matter. We hope it results in a less formal working environment for us all.

Respectfully.

_____, *Director of Human Resources*
_____, *Director of Counselling Services*

The CommunicAID Board of Trustees approved this proposal in principle, with the caution that acceptable dress must be clearly defined so that it can be enforced. They will review the code at their next meeting with a view toward announcing it in the next employee newsletter.

News writing

Background for Exercise 9-4

*F*ollowing are excerpts from last night's meeting of the CommunicAID Board of Directors. They have been given to you because the Board wants publicity on this new venture.

1. The CommunicAID Board of Trustees voted by a 9-3 margin to sign a contract with Anytown, YS to purchase the former elementary school property located on Mercer Street. The purchase price has been negotiated at $2.5 million.

   Sources of Funding:

   $500,000 grant........YourState Housing Authority. 50% of this grant is restricted to removing asbestos and lead paint from the school basement.

   $250,000 grant........Anytown City Council.

   Low interest loan ....Through a federal facilities improvements fund administered by the Department of Housing and Urban Development (HUD).

   The architectural firm of Anderson and Lee, of Anytown, has been named chief architect for the project. Tenders will be requested this week for all construction tasks and work will begin within two months.

   Plans for the new facility:
   * A satellite office for CommunicAID staff operating in the Mercer Street area.
   * Office space for non-profit affiliates of CommunicAID
   * Conference rooms for community education and meetings
   * Counselling rooms at which CommunicAID and affiliate counselors can meet with individual clients
   * 32-bed overnight shelter
   * 60-person day shelter with food service
   * 30-person long-term family shelter
   * 12,000 square foot food pantry

What does this mean to CommunicAID?

The following information will help you determine what public relations strategy, if any, should be pursued as the result of this announcement.

1. The Mercer school has been empty for two years. This Anytown City Council chose to divest itself of the school building rather than hold it for future educational development.

2. Mercer Street is on the opposite side of Anytown from the present CommunicAID offices and programs. Once a thriving largely blue-collar neighborhood, the area has been particularly hard hit by the closure of several Anytown manufacturing plants. It has a population of elderly and low-income families, many of whom are in need of support for food and housing. Mercer area schools are the lowest-performing in the Anytown region. An adjacent area known for crime and drug trafficking is seen to be rapidly encroaching on the Mercer Street area.

Continued

Because of its success in coordinating services for a similarly disadvantaged population in its current location, CommunicAID was given the option to purchase the property.

CommunicAID research shows that the Mercer Street population is unaware of the services available from CommunicAID. In addition, the lack of public transport would make it difficult for the Mercer residents to reach the current CommunicAID offices.

2. You may expect opposition from two local groups, the Citizens for Literacy which had been lobbying the City Council to transform the school to a library and remedial education center, and "NIMBY", a local group opposing the project on the basis that it will bring an influx of indigent people into what is an already depressed area.

3. The Chairman of the CommunicAID Board will be unavailable for a press conference until next week, so you will have to make the announcement via press release. The Director of Public Affairs will be available to make a comment if necessary. What effect will this have on the likelihood that the release will be printed?

4. The Mayor of Anytown hailed the vote.

5. Proof of local residency will be required to access services at the Mercer Street Center.

Feature writing
Background for Exercises 10-2

CommunicAID management wants a feature story related to the Mercer Street Center in its annual report to the Anytown community. Management believes this article will add a "human interest" element to what is often perceived as a cold, finance-centered document.

You may choose to write about the center as a whole or about a project or activity related to one of its affiliate organizations. Your article should focus on a person or the people who have been involved in or benefited from one or more of these programs. The following highlights will get you started on a theme for the article. You will make up the details to develop an interesting feature.

Highlights of the first year of the Mercer Street Satellite Center

- The first Sunday of every month is an "open house" at which Anytown residents are invited to tour the center and to hear lectures on the programs and volunteer opportunities.

- The Key Club at Anytown High School adopted the Mercer Food Pantry as their project for the year. They conducted fundraisers and food drives and received favorable publicity for the club and the Food Pantry for their creative ideas.

- The Communication Honor Society at Central College adopted the homeless shelter as their project for the year, challenging all other departmental honor societies at the college to outdo them in collecting toiletries, and other items needed by the shelter on a daily basis.

- The local newspaper has given CommunicAID a monthly column in which to list volunteer opportunities for CommunicAID and its affiliates at both of its facilities.

- 75 percent of the students who received tutoring in math and reading at the Mercer center passed to the next grade. This compares to 50% of students who did not receive tutoring.

- Under a grant from the YourState Housing Authority, Homes for All completed renovation on a 12-apartment block in January. All apartments were occupied immediately by families in temporary residence at the Family Shelter.

Mercer Center Statistics — First Year of Operation

		# staff	# volunteers	# people served
*	Mercer Center Food Bank	15	50	3,500 **
*	Mercer Center Homeless Shelters			
	Overnight Shelter	15	30	6,125 **
	Day Shelter and food service	35	100	12,765 **
	Family Shelter	10	25	135
*	Mercer Center Literacy Program	10	350	300
*	Homes for All	25	75	680
*	Back-to-Work Training/Job Placement	20	100	375

**   NOTE: The numbers for the food bank, overnight and day shelters are the total number of visits to these centers. Some people may have accessed more than one of these services and/or used the services multiple times. The numbers for the Family Shelter, Literacy Program, Homes for All and Back to Work programs do not include multiple visits.

Spokespersons

The following people could be expected to be the subject of this article and/or who would comment for this article, depending on the topic and theme you choose to pursue. It is your responsibility to select the appropriate spokespersons and to write any quotes from them. Next to each person we have identified the attitude this person would likely have toward the project. This attitude should be reflected in his or her words.

Except for CommunicAID personnel and the mayor (whom you have previously identified), you may name any of the people. You may assume that anyone in an official capacity has agreed that his or her name may be used, but it is possible some of the private citizens may not wish to be named. How can you deal with this?

*   CommunicAID president ....Positive; credit staff, city, community; aware of public relations opportunity, mission-driven

*   CommunicAID program director..............Positive; credit staff and affiliates

*   Anytown Mayor ....Enthusiastic; political; take some credit

*   Presidents of relevant affiliates ....Positive; appreciative, forward-looking

*   Spokespersons for groups that ....Positive; mission-driven
       provided support for CommunicAID

*   Spokespersons for groups that ....Cautious; unwilling to give full support
       opposed the center   but worst fears have not been realized

*   Volunteers ....Enthusiastic; positive; inspired

*   Mercer residents who have ....Willing to tell their stories, appreciative of people
       participated as clients in the programs   who have helped them; optimistic.

Newsletters

Backgkround for Exercises 10-4 and 10-5

You are responsible for producing two quarterly newsletters: an "internal" newsletter for the employees of CommunicAID and its affiliated agencies and an "external" newsletter for the Anytown general public.

The following stories are the raw material for both newsletters – the first issues in the new calendar year. They include possible articles representing every department and agency. Note: this is an ideal situation. In the real world, you are more likely to have departments that never release information. Some of the items will go in both newsletters, others only in one. Some may not be appropriate and/or timely for either.

Completing the worksheet for this assignment will help you determine which articles to include in each newsletter. Be aware that these items are presented as you might have received them. They are not necessarily grammatical or consistent in style. That is your job. Also, you may want additional details to flesh out a story. If so, you may assume you have contacted the relevant people and have obtained the information and/or quotes that you need. NOTE you may name the people in any blank.

Dress code:..........................It has been approved as you wrote it. Now you need to tell the staff.

President's Message: ....She wants a draft article, "something topical and of interest to staff".

Mercer Center: ....The news story you wrote in Exercise 9-4 will be the basis for the lead news story for the newsletters. Exercise 10-5 will guide you through adapting this story to newsletter style.

Volunteer of the Year: ....Scheduling clerk _____ was named "Volunteer of the Year" at the annual volunteers' holiday party. HR received more favorable comments on her than on anyone else. She is a life-long resident of Anytown. She started volunteering in1995 when she retired after 40 years teaching kindergarten and raising her own family of four. She arranges for needy and homeless clients to meet with affiliates and CommunicAID personnel. *If you want to write a feature on her, do so.*

Births: ....*Following are two notices you saw on the bulletin board in the staff room:*
_____ had a baby girl, Sarah Jane.24" long, 8 lbs. 9 oz. Her boyfriend is _____. _____, and his wife had a baby girl. She's beautiful."

Weddings: ....*(You may make up as appropriate).*

Engagements:.....................*Following is a phone message from Sandy in accounting: "_____ got engaged. The ring is huge! Can it go in the newsletter?"*

Accounting News:...............W-2 tax forms will be out to all employees by the end of the month. Questions to _____ in the accounting office.

Softball Sign-Ups: ...._____ wants us to field a team in the Anytown slow-pitch softball league-amateur division, this summer. Games are Mondays and Wednesdays June 1 - July 15. Teams are 10-members each (including four outfielders) and we must have

From Affiliates: ...._____, one of the literacy program students, received the most improved student award for the second quarter at Elms Elementary school.

....Renovations are done on the Elms Apartments. All 12 have been occupied by families from the Family Shelter. There was a big celebration to open them on moving day. It's a Homes for All project.

....The Food Bank got a big load of groceries from the kids at Anytown High School.

....As you know, the winter has been really cold. All of the shelters have been overflowing for the whole month. The supplies donated by Central College have been very welcome. They conducted some sort of challenge to get them.

Newsletter Staff: ....Editor - You

New Employees: ...._____ graduated in December from YourState University. He worked last year as a summer intern with CommunicAID affiliate Homes for All. He will work with Joann Drummond on the Mercer Street project.

...._____ – webmaster for CommunicAID and affiliates.

Fundraising time ahead: ......The annual CommunicAID fundraising month is April. This is the fundraising for CommunicAID services, such as facilities and communications. *(It does NOT benefit the programs or affiliates directly).* The schedule includes:

- ....Kickoff luncheon for CommunicAID staff and committee members April 2nd at Mercer Center.

- ....5 mile public road race through Anytown Park. April 7th. Sign up and additional information from the Public Affairs Office.

- ....Benefit dinner April 19th at the Civic Center. $100/per person. *Honorees and/or guest speaker of your choice.*

- ....Community phon-a-thon April 24 using phone bank at Central College Development office.

- ....To encourage staff participation and make the campaign fun for all, there will again be prizes to the department that raises the most funds (outside of the official functions) and that has the most creative fundraising project. Can anyone top the planning department's "board-napping" of the CommunicAID Directors from their April meeting last year?

Schedule of events: ....*(Youl may determine)*

Cartoon: ....You receive the following memo from a staff member in the Literacy program. "Found this cartoon in my file the other day. Hope it is clear enough for you to use." *Note: the cartoon is very clear, but should you use it?*

Suggestions: ....The following was in the Suggestion Box last month. "I think we should have a special recognition for the Employee of the Month. How about reserving the parking spot closest to the door for a month?"

Resources: ....Create an ongoing list of web sites and/or summary of articles that CommunicAID staff will find useful.

Crisis writing

Background for Exercises 12-1, 12-2 and 12-3

Sometimes it is necessary to publicly address issues that may embarrass or otherwise show your employer in a "less than favorable" light. Many public companies have been faced with this situation when their administrators were charged with financial malfeasance, processes were shown to be environmentally irresponsible or promotions suspected of deliberately violating "truth in advertising" laws, for example. Following is a scenario in which you must publicly address a situation that has the potential to impact relationships with one or more of your organization's key publics.

Important Background Information

CommunicAID has always prided itself on the level of support it receives from the Anytown community. Annual fund contributions have nearly doubled over the last three years as citizens responded to requests to "join a partnership for a better community."

The Development Office (i.e., fundraising office) has put special effort into developing donor incentive programs and especially into cultivating local industries and several high-profile, wealthy citizens as the foundation for a capital campaign that CommunicAID plans to launch in three months on behalf of its affiliate Homes for All. The capital campaign will fund the purchase and renovation of 12 abandoned properties on a six-block section of downtown Anytown. Homes for All estimates that, when renovated, the properties will provide homes for 85 low income families. It will be the largest fundraising campaign ever undertaken by CommunicAID. The campaign theme will be under the theme of "families helping families."

The Situation:

Two months ago, CommunicAID development officer Albert Mathison was terminated for falsifying expense reports. Now, on the eve of the capital campaign, a disgruntled Mathison has written a letter to the editor of the Anytown daily newspaper. The letter charges the CommunicAID administration with "extravagant expenditures" including luxury dinners and annual administrator "retreats" at five-star holiday resorts. Mathison claims that these expenditures were made possible by diverting a percentage of the contributions made to the fundraising campaigns of CommunicAID affiliates into the CommunicAID president's "discretionary budget".

The newspaper editor has assigned a reporter to follow up on the charges and determine if they are true and if it is indeed a story. The reporter intends to file the story with or without CommunicAID comment. Your inquiries show that the story is indeed true. As Mathison discovered after a casual conversation with a Literacy program coordinator who was bemoaning the "disappearance" of a critical budget item, part of the literacy fund had been put under the control of the CommunicAID president's assistant. The account is funded from the money raised through annual fund campaigns and is being used to pay for the items Mathison mentioned. Your subsequent conversations with other affiliates reveals the same thing regarding their budgets.

Reaction: The CommunicAID president's reaction is that all funds have been accounted for (which is true) and that he uses the account to effectively develop contacts who will contribute to future projects for both CommunicAID and its affiliates. A case in point is the current capital campaign for which CommunicAID has already secured $5 million in donations from a charitable foundation and two Anytown businessmen. The relationships on which these donations are made, he argues, cannot be developed by mail or over a cup of coffee.

Also, you know that the staff retreat in question was held at the lakeside estate of a board member who offers the facility to all of the charitable organizations she supports.

Persuasive messages

Background to Exercises 14-2, 14-3 and 14-4

This background information will be used for three assignments in Chapter Fourteen. It is a scenario in which CommmunicAID might feel compelled to issue a persuasive message.

NOTE: Central College, another of the text clients, will be writing in opposition to your message. For the "Letter to the Editor" assignment you should assume that the Anytown newspaper has printed an editorial supporting higher education as the funding that should be retained.

The Situation:

The economic crisis in YourState has not abated, and Governor _____ continues to make cuts in the grants to non-profit and educational institutions. CommunicAID and its affiliates receive a large percentage of their funding through subsidies and grants from YourState government agencies. The most recent round of cuts reduced their administrative budgets by over $600,000, and rumors abound that more cuts will come. Word on the street is that the cuts will hit either higher education or social services for the needy and homeless.

These cuts have already impacted the staffing levels for several of the affiliate programs and additional cuts will likely result in reduced hours or levels of operation for some of them. The cuts have also affected the ability of CommunicAID to increase fundraising activities in the private sector that would reduce the effect of the cuts to the affiliates.

You have been working with the team that is developing the organization's response to these cuts. Among other tactics, you have recommended that CommunicAID should make a greater effort to persuade the Anytown legislative representatives to vote against any cuts to social services and to carry your message to the governor and state legislature.

You have recommended a two-pronged strategy: contacting the legislators directly; and persuading the Anytown community to add its voice to your cause. The CommunicAID president and affiliates have all agreed and directed you to draft the first letters in this campaign. *Note: You are free to determine some details of the effects of the cuts, but do not assume that the programs are in danger of closing based on current projections.*

For this project, you may write on behalf of CommunicAID or any of the affiliates. What are the advantages and disadvantages to each strategy?

Trade Fairs and Conferences

Background for Exercise16-8

CommunicAID has been invited to participate in the annual "Community Awareness Conference and Fair" sponsored by the Anytown Mayor's Office and Chamber of Commerce. The one-day conference will bring together community business, civic and social services leaders to discuss how they can raise community awareness of the needs and services available to disadvantaged populations in the community.

The Fair is the public arm of this project. It is open to the greater Anytown public and is typically attended by over 7,500 people each year, 35 percent of whom are children. Booths at the fair are sponsored by social services and civic organizations that want to get their names in front of the public and to recruit volunteers and donors. This year's fair theme is "Get involved."

Community Awareness Fair Specifics

<u>Details:</u> ....Dates: Oct. 17 (4–8 p.m.) and Saturday Oct. 18 (9 a.m.–8 p.m.)

......Location: Anytown Civic Center, Anytown, YS

......Theme: The theme for the fair will be "Get involved"

<u>Display Details:</u> Booths:......8' x 8' spaces, Booth #34 at the conference will be reserved as the conference information booth.

Standard: ......Each booth will include one 3' x 6' table with gray skirt plus gray backdrop, three electric outlets.

Extras: ......Television and video monitors, VCRs at additional cost

Food Service: ......Coffee, tea, soft drinks and sandwiches will be available at designated locations throughout the fair.

Program: ......Conference organizers produce a program that includes a listing of the names and addresses of all vendors. They will also accept ads for this program.

<u>Vendor Schedule:</u> ......The official drawing for any prizes offered by individual vendors will be held at the information booth at 6 p.m. on Saturday evening.

<u>Media Coverage:</u> ......_____ TV Channel #____ will broadcast live throughout the Friday and Saturday evening news shows. Typically they will feature live action with booth holders that have activities or interesting give-aways, especially for children.

......The Anytown newspaper will also likely send a reporter and photographer as soon as the Fair opens on Friday for the Saturday edition.

......The Anytown newspaper annual supplement on non-profit organizations and volunteer opportunities is published in September, two weeks before the Fair, and advertising space is available.

<u>CommunicAID Focus:</u> ......This will be the primary public promotion of the year for CommunicAID. Your purpose in attending this conference and fair is to promote CommunicAID and its affiliates. For this year, the focus will be on the Mercer Street Center, which is still growing and in need of volunteers. You have access to all CommunicAID and affiliates' equipment and services and can stage any demonstrations, tests etc. that relate to your theme and that are practical in a public arena.

......CommunicAID management believes that the educational brochure you have already created can be used for this conference, as can the seven-minute video production filmed at the center.

1000 West Main Street, Anytown, YS 11111
Telephone: 1-800-000-0000, Fax: 1-444-000-0001
Website: xxx.healthway.com

Dear New Staff Member:

Welcome to HealthWay Pharmacies, Inc. HealthWay is one of the largest and most successful chain of pharmacies in YourState, and I hope you will find your career with us rewarding.

We like to think of HealthWay Pharmacies as an "employee-friendly" company. We make it a practice, whenever possible, to promote from within, thereby keeping career paths open for our current employees. Over 70 percent of our current supervisors and most of the managers started out with our company. Several of them began as interns with us.

For your part, we ask that you focus on the job you were employed to do. Since Jack and I founded HealthWay, we have achieved remarkable growth, largely through the efforts of our dedicated employees. By keeping sales staff focused on sales and customer service staff focused on responding to the public, for example, we can make the most of every opportunity. Of course the people who come into our pharmacies and access our mail, on-line or telephone prescription service are the most important concern for us all. They should be able to have 100% confidence in our high standards for both quality and service ... and that is up to you!

Please read the enclosed staffing and policy manual thoroughly. It contains information about benefits and company policies that you must know. If you have any additional questions, please feel free to ask your immediate supervisor or a member of the Human Resources Department.

We encourage you to express your opinion and contribute ideas regarding our procedures and practices: suggestion boxes are hung in every break room and we try to respond to as many suggestions as possible in the monthly staff newsletter.

Again, on behalf of the entire HealthWay management team, I welcome you to our company and I hope you enjoy working with us.

Sincerely,

Marsha Robinson
Chairman and CEO

Current Year Corporate Goals

These goals were adopted at the beginning of the financial year by the executive committee. They are based on projections from department heads and the 10-year corporate plan.

- Increase gross revenues by 20 percent.

- Expand services to NextState by opening pharmacies in four suburbs of the NextState city closest to Anytown.

- Secure contracts to provide by-mail prescription services to the members of the state health plans of both YourState and NextState.

- Launch on-line "ask your pharmacist" service.

Current Year Department Goals
(set by departments to help the corporation meet its corporate goals)

Sales goal ....Secure contracts with YourState and NextState health systems for Mail-Meds program.

....Attend NextState health fairs to introduce HealthWay services.

Customer Service goal ....In-store: Reduce complaints about in-store services by 10%.

....Mail-Meds: Respond to all customer contacts within 24 hours.

Public Relations goal ....Put HealthWay "on the map" in NextState.

....Develop monthly newsletter for YourState residents.

....Raise public awareness of HealthWay's community involvement.

Training goal................................Initiate monthly training for in-store staff.

Information Services (IS) goal ..Execute technical specifications for "ask your pharmacist" service.

Management goal ....Secure funding to support expansion into NextState.

....Develop relationships with leaders of NextState communities.

Memberships: **National Pharmaceutical Association:** Association of national, regional and individual pharmacies. Represents the retail pharmaceutical industry in Washington. Provides education and training services for member companies.

YourState Association of Pharmacies: Represents retail pharamacies at state level. Provides educational, legal and business consulting services to members.

Anytown Chamber of Commerce: For the purpose of this text, the Chamber of Commerce with which you will work is the Chamber of Commerce serving the community in which your campus is located (or the nearest Chamber of Commerce).

PROFILE
About the Company

Offices:	Address:	# Staff
Corporate Office	1000 Main Street West, Mansfield Towers, Anytown, YS 11111 *Executives; Communications; Accounting and Payment Processing; Corporate Training; Retail Division/Customer Service; Marketing.*	65
Pharmacies	165 locations throughout YourState including all major centers. All of these locations provide full walk-in and/or drive-through pharmacy services staffed by registered pharmacists, as well as retail facilities for beauty and healthcare, hygiene and home products.	2,475
Prescriptions	Box 919, Othertown, YS 11111 This facility is dedicated to the Mail-Meds program. It includes an order department for telephone, mail, fax and e-mail prescription orders, a customer service department, a processing department staffed by registered pharmacy technicians, and a shipping department.	80

Owners:

Marsha Robinson	51 percent*	Jack Robinson	15 percent
Edwin Riley	15 percent	John Campbell	10 percent
Peter McMillan	10 percent		

*   *The fact that Ms. Robinson owns 51 percent of the company allows HealthWay to take advantage of contracting opportunities for women-owned companies.*

History: HealthWay was founded in 1985 when Marsha and Jack Robinson, owners of Anytown Drugs, purchased the assets of Anytown pharmacies Riley Drugs and Campbell Rx. They have continued to expand throughout YourState, providing pharmacy services to many small communities as well as urban areas and developing a reputation for supporting the communities in which they operate.

Three years ago, faced with the prospect of closing several of the smallest, least profitable stores, HealthWay invested in the technology to provide prescription services by mail. Today, hundreds of thousands of YourState residents order medications by mail, phone, fax or e-mail and receive them by mail. HealthWay plans to expand its services throughout the region, beginning with NextState.

Retail: HealthWay is one of the three largest pharmacy chains in YourState.

Refill: Through its Mail-Meds service HealthWay provides medications by mail to the members of the health insurance plans of 345 companies and organizations. The largest clients include the employee health plan for Central College and the health plan for the YourState Firefighters' Association.

Individuals without health insurance or whose health insurer is not a HealthWay client, can access HealthWay prescription services on a cash basis.

HealthWay Pharmacies Inc.

PROFILE
Corporate organization chart
Relevant web sites

BOARD OF TRUSTEES

CHAIRMAN - - - - - - - - - - - - External Corporate Counsel
Marsha Robinson

PRESIDENT/CEO
Jack Robinson

VP - OPERATIONS
Edwin Riley

GENERAL MANAGERS
Allan Mitchell, *Retail*
Philip Anderson, *Mail-Meds*

DIR - Information Systems (IS)
Peter Blake
Lead Programmer
Programmers
Operators
Data clerks

CORP. TRAINING MGR.
Maureen Johns

VP - ADMIN/FINANCE
John Campbell

ACCOUNTANT
Alison Johnson
Payment Processing
Payroll
Billing

DIR - Human Resources
Sandra Riley
Recruitment Spec.
Benefits Spec.
HR clerks

DIR- Records and Quality
Control.

**VP - SALES, MARKETING AND
PUBLIC RELATIONS**
Jeff Marshall

DIR - SALES
Sara McLean
Sales Representatives
Sales clerical

DIR - CUSTOMER SERVICE (CS)
CS Representatives - Clients
CS Representatives - Customers
CS clerical

DIR - MARKETING
Proposal Specialist
Marketing Specialists
Marketing clerical

DIR - PUBLIC RELATIONS
Roy Adams and (Your name)
Public Relations Writers
Desktop Publishing Specialist

Web sites:

American Pharmacists Association: <http://www.aphanet.org>
Directory of State Pharmacy Associations: <http://www.nacds.org>
U.S. Department of Health and Human Services: <http://www.dhhs.gov>
U.S. Food and Drug Administration: <http://www.fda.gov>

PROFILE
Financial information and growth statistics

Financials and Growth Statistics:

Summary of Financial Information

	This Year	Last Year
INCOME		
Revenue from retail operations	$6,000,000	$4,000,000
Revenue from "Mail-Meds" services	1,500,000	500,000
Total Income	$7,500,000	$4,500,000
EXPENSES		
Staff (salaries, commissions, insurance, 401K)	$ 4,530,000	$3,080,000
Facilities (rent, insurance, maintenance)	800,000	200,000
Computer expenses	800,000	600,000
Memberships	20,000	10,000
Advertising and promotion	550,000	50,000
Other	150,000	60,000
Total Expenses	$ 6,850,000	$4,000,000
NET OPERATING PROFIT (Income-Expenses)	$ **650,000**	$ **500,000**

Growth in Total Staff Numbers

6 years ago 500
5 years ago 700
4 years ago 1,100
3 years ago 1,500
2 years ago 1,920
Last year 2,400
This year 2,620

Growth in Mail-Meds Contracts

N/A
N/A
N/A
3 years ago 35
2 years ago 90
Last year 185
This year 345

Media History: Press Releases issued last year:

Jeff Marshall promoted to VP Sales and Marketing.

HealthWay to open new pharmacy in _____ (name of town – 15 such releases issued throughout YourState during the year).

Office Hours: HealthWAY retail stores are open Monday–Sunday from 7 am to 10 pm.

All employees are assigned to units comprised of at least one pharmacist, two pharmacy technicians, and six sales clerks. Each unit works a staggered 40-hour schedule per week. This ensures that customers can access all retail and pharmacy services. On normal weeks, this staggered schedule will comprise four 10-hour days, alternating between an early (7 am-3:30 pm) and late (1:30 pm-10 pm) schedule. Work schedules are posted for each month at the beginning of the month.

* All store managers must be available for a weekly managers' telephone conference currently scheduled at 1:30 p.m. every Monday.

* All units must be available for bi-weekly unit meetings/training on a schedule to be announced at the beginning of each month.

* As required by state law, HealthWay provides employees with two half-hour unpaid "meal" breaks and two 15-minute breaks during each 10-hour workday. Staff are assigned meal breaks to ensure that all positions are covered during all working hours.

Personal Space: All employees will be assigned a locker for personal effects during working hours. HealthWay is not responsible for the safety or security of any personal objects you bring to the store.

Break Room: Each store has a break room in which we provide unlimited coffee, tea and hot chocolate mix for all staff. It is the responsibility of staff members who drink coffee to ensure that fresh coffee is brewed whenever the pot is empty. Bottled water is also available and a vending machine for soda and for candy and snacks is located in the break room.

Staff may also keep their own food and beverages in the refrigerator and heat food in the microwave. All dirty dishes should be washed out by the employee. Cleaning staff have been instructed to dispose of dirty dishes left in the break room overnight.

Long Service: The company annually honors staff who have reached three, five and ten years of service during the calendar year. Awards are as follows:

Three years — company pin

Five years — engraved pen

Ten years — clock.

Background to Writing Assignments: HealthWay Pharmacies

Following is background information you will need for some of the writing exercises in this workbook. Instructions for the exercises can be found in the Part Two of the workbook.

Organizational Culture
Background to Exercise 4-2

Since its beginning, HealthWay has required all female retail store staff to wear smocks. Males are required to wear white shirts with ties. The aim is to provide a common, professional "look" and to make it easy for customers to identify staff to assist them. Because pharmacists and pharmacy technicians also wear smocks or white shirts and ties, this gave equal requirements for all store personnel.

However, over the last year, the human relations department has found it increasingly difficult to recruit non-pharmacy staff for the retail stores, especially those in urban and suburban areas. The HR department conducted a survey of current staff and applicants for the retail positions and learned that the smocks were a liability. Young applicants (who traditionally fill 35% of the sales clerk positions) find them particularly distasteful. Customers say the smocks give the store a "dated" atmosphere instead of the up-to-date image that management wants to portray. Comments on the regulations ranged from "ugly," "I don't even own a tie," "looks like something my grandmother would wear," and "even my grandmother wouldn't wear that," to "no way I'm going to wear that."

To remedy this situation, the HR department has recommended to management that non-pharmacist retail staff be allowed to dress in street clothes (with some limitations). They must also wear a nametag with the HealthWay logo and their name. HealthWay management has agreed in principle, but wants to see a draft of the actual policy. This is your task.

Management has raised the following concerns, which you should consider in your policy. Be aware that *not* making it clear will result in problems.

- Nothing that would be considered recreational or beach wear.
- Attire must be professional. (What does this mean? Remember that HealthWay employs retail staff of all ages, sexes and ethnic groups.)
- Staff must be able to perform all jobs, including stocking shelves (both high and low) while looking professional.
- Some members of management are concerned that nametags alone will not differentiate staff from customers. Can you suggest a compromise?

Newswriting

Background to Exercise 9-4

Good News! The president of HealthWay Pharmacies, Inc. has just received the following letter from the director of the YourState State Employees Health System.

YourState State Employees
Association

Ms. Marsha Robinson
Chairman
HealthWay Pharmacies, Inc.
100 West Main Street
Anytown, YS 11111

Dear Ms. Robinson:

Congratulations! The YourState State Employees Association (YSEA) is pleased to notify you that HealthWay Pharmacies, Inc. has been chosen to provide prescription services by mail to members of the YSEA Health system for the next four years. Our attorneys will send a contract for your signature within two weeks. On receipt of the signed document, we shall notify our members and you may begin promoting your services to them.

As stipulated in the YSEA Request for Proposal (RFP), our operations staff will conduct quarterly on-site reviews at the HealthWay prescription handling facility. Our particular aims will be to ensure the timeliness and quality of your prescription handling and billing systems and your procedures for maintaining complete patient confidentiality.

We shall review both the company and YSEA complaint logs related to your company's prescription handling. We shall expect senior management of the facililty and, on request, of the company to be present at these meetings. Deficiency in any of these areas may be grounds for YSEA to notify our members of your lapse and/or to discontinue the contract.

Ms. Joanne Rogers, contracting officer, has been assigned as liaison with your company to answer questions regarding this contract. If you require any assistance from our office, please contact her at (200) 929-0744.

Sincerely,

J.D. Markham
Director, YSEA

What does this news mean to HealthWay Pharmacies, Inc?

1. This is the first time that YSEA has offered its members a mail-prescription service. There are over 1 million state employees who are members of this system. Potentially this could mean a doubling of HealthWay's mail-in service ("Mail-Meds") over the next two years.

2. The proposal HealthWay submitted commits HealthWay to maintaining a completely separate record-keeping and processing facility for YSEA member requests. HealthWay routinely maintains separate record-keeping for each of its clients and prides itself on the quality of its record-

keeping, so this is not a problem. To achieve this HealthWay will move its entire prescription handling facility to new premises in Othertown, YS. This building will be divided to provide space for two separate processing departments with a common shipping department which meets YSEA requirements. This will allow HealthWay to further automate its shipping department and take advantage of bulk shipping rates with several carriers.

3.   HealthWay has received financial support for the new facility from the YourState Office of Economic Development under the governor's "New Jobs; New Opportunities" initiative. The new facility is expected to employ 40 additional staff in non-professional categories as well as licensed pharmacists and pharmacy technicians.

4.   Establishing the new facility is likely to delay by six months the development of an online "ask your pharmacist" program that the company had expected to launch next month.

<u>Other Information:</u>

The following people have agreed to be quoted in the release. You may draft quotes for any or all of them as appropriate.

•   J.D. Smith, Director of the Health Insurance Division of the YourState State Employees Association

•   Linda McManus, Director of the YourState Office of Economic Development

•   Peter Simson, Mayor of Othertown, YS.

Feature writing

Background to Exercise 10-2

The following information is the raw material for a feature story that HealthWay management wants to use in the annual report it produces for clients and insurance providers. Management believes this article will add some "human interest" to the report while providing an opportunity to promote the company's excellent record for regulatory compliance and customer satisfaction. The basis of the story is the YourState State Employees Association (YSEA) contract on which HealthWay began work one year ago and on which you previously wrote a news release. The information below should give you a wide range of options for writing this story.

Statistics on YSEA prescription processing and customer service

	# Prescriptions filled	# Customer Service inquiries
First Quarter	714	214
Second Quarter	1,448	365
Third Quarter*	6,674	360
Fourth Quarter	4,771	168

* *Flu season*

Highlights of the first year of providing Mail-Meds services to YSEA

■ Mail-Meds services began for YSEA members 12 months ago from new premises in Othertown, YS.

■ YSEA members who signed up for the program were given address, phone, fax, e-mail and customer service numbers and addresses specifically for their program.

■ The first YSEA customer was a single mother from outside Ruraltown with a diabetic child and two jobs.

■ 35% of the people who enrollled in the service are members of the YSEA retirees health program.

■ The number of prescriptions for YSEA members peaked in November during the flu season which was especially virulent.

■ The customer service log shows the following:

- 50% of the contacts were inquiries on prescription status

- 20% of the contacts related to billing issues

- 30% of the contacts were complaints. Of these, 80% related to an inability to access the website, 15% related to mail service, and 5% complained about HealthWay services or products.

- HealthWay easily passed all of the YSEA quality control inspections

■ A YSEA survey of comparative prescription costs indicated that for 20 of the most common medications, the unit cost of the 90-day supply of prescriptions ordered through the HealthWay Mail-Meds program was 25% below the unit cost of the same medications purchased on a 30-day basis from walk-in pharmacies.

Spokespersons

The following people could be expected to be the subject of this article and/or comment for this article, depending on the topic and theme you choose to pursue. It is your responsibility to select the appropriate spokespersons and to write any quotes from them. Next to each person we have identified the attitude this person would likely have toward the project. This attitude should be reflected in his or her words.

Except for the HealthWay personnel and the mayor (whom you have already identified), you may name any of the people. You may assume that anyone in an official capacity has agreed that his or her name may be used, but it is possible some of the private citizens may not wish to be named. How can you deal with this?

Spokespersons	Attitude, message themes
• HealthWay president	Positive; credit staff, city; aware of the public relations opportunity, mission-driven
* Mail-Meds VP and QC director	Positive; credit staff and affiliates
* Othertown Mayor	Enthusiastic; political; take some credit
* YSEA Director of Health Insurance	Positive; forward-looking
* Customers	Willing to tell their stories, generally enthusiastic
* Mail-Meds customer service staff	Willing to tell stories

Newsletters

Background to Exercises 10-4 and 10-5

The following stories are the raw material for a client newsletter and an employee newsletter — the first issues after the new year. They include possible articles representing every HealthWay department.. *Note: this is an ideal situation. In the real world, you are more likely to have departments that never release any information.* Some of the items will go in both newsletters, others only in one. Completing the exercise in the text for this assignment will help you determine which articles to include in each newsletter.

Be aware that these items are presented "as you received them." They are not necessarily grammatical or consistent in style. That is your job. You should fill in the blanks with names and places you know.

<u>Dress code:</u> .... The new policy has been approved as you wrote it. *(Note: The Human Resources Director is concerned that staff will react badly to this policy and that work time will be lost while they complain about it).* What tone should you take? Why? Can you think of another way to handle the subject?

<u>YSEA contract:</u> .... The news story you wrote in Exercise 9-4 will be the basis for the lead news story for the newsletters. Exercise 10-5 will guide you through adapting this story to newsletter style.

<u>President's Message:</u> .... She wants suggestions on a topic for this month.

<u>Office News</u> .... *(Note: In real life, you will get this type of information from branch correspondents, even managers. What to use is always a tough decision without hurting anyone's feelings or discouraging future contributions. This is a good time to remember who pays your salary.)*

Yourstate/Head Office: .... Holiday party: We had a formal dinner at the Hotel Marquese. The hotel was beautiful and everyone looked great. Even Joe Smith minded his manners for the evening.

North Region Stores: .... Our Christmas party was a theme party at Wild West Village in _____. Great party! Everybody went and Manager _____ showed up as Jesse James, complete with six-shooter. We always knew he was a bandit.

South Region Stores: .... We had a family picnic at _____ on December 12th. The highlight was the appearance of Santa Claus in a _____. He had candy for all the kids and flowers for all the ladies. Thanks to management for sponsoring the party and to our president and CEO, Angela and Jack, for coming. "Y'all come back now."

Mai-Meds: .... The Mail-Meds third shift processing group set a new record for volume of prescriptions filled without error last month. They filled 10% more prescriptions than the previous record by any group.

<u>Births:</u> .... *Following is a notice you saw on the bulletin board in the coffee room: "_____ had a baby. Her husband is _____"* *You also received the following from the Othertown Store: "_____, pharmacist, and his girlfriend _____ had a baby girl, _____."*

<u>Engagements:</u> *Following is a phone message from "Sandy" in Sometown: "_____ got engaged. The ring is huge! Can it go in the newsletter?"*

<u>Continued</u>

<u>Accounting News:</u>	We will have W-2 tax forms out to all employees by the end of the month. If you have any questions refer them to the Accounting Office, extension 555.

<u>Weddings:</u> _____ (customer service) to _____
_____ (sales clerk,) to _____

<u>Illness:</u> _____ father is recovering from surgery.
_____ son _____, broke his leg playing soccer

<u>Regulations</u>

Following is a note from VP Operations re: Privacy

We have heard through the American Pharmaceutical Association that a store in SouthState is being sued for $9 million because a customer service representative released confidential information about a patient. We remind all staff that maintaining privacy of medical records is both a requirement and a principle of HealthWay's commitment to our clients and our customers.

PERSONAL NOTE TO YOU, THE EDITOR: "In addition to this being an important issue, I want to be <u>seen</u> to be reviewing these regulations with our staff. It is always a good tactic to have "public" proof that we keep them reminded of the need for privacy." — Ed Riley.

<u>IS News:</u> With the help of sales and customer service reps,HealthWay programmers have nearly completed the special programming for the YSEA contract and will be testing it against actual numbers during the next few weeks.

<u>Cartoon:</u> You receive the following note scrawled on a fax from the Illinois GM:
"Found this cartoon in my file the other day. Hope it is clear enough for you to use."
Note: the cartoon is very clear.

<u>NPA Note:</u> The National Pharmacy Association (NPA)has sent a memo asking pharmaceutical companies to remind their clients that Congress is preparing new legislation on the privacy of medical records. The Secretary of Health and Human Services is seeking comments from parties in the pharmaceutical industry regarding changes that need to be made. The deadline is February 15th. Please encourage clients to send their comments to the NPA.

<u>Newsletter Staff:</u> Editor - You
Office Correspondents: North Region Stores: _____
West Region Stores: _____
South Region Stores: _____
Mail-Meds: _____

<u>New Employees:</u> _____ - Sales representative
_____ - Pharmacy technician - Sometown
_____ - Pharmacy technician - Othertown

<u>Suggestions:</u> The following were found in the Suggestion Box during the last month.

"I think we should have a special recognition for the sales clerk in each region. How about giving a half day off for that person each month?"

"I think the duties of the cleaning lady should be extended to wash the dirty dishes, as long as they are left in the sink before close of business each night."

Crisis Writing

Background to Exercises 12-1, 12-2 and 12-3

Sometimes it is necessary to publicly address issues that may embarrass or otherwise show your employer in a "less than favorable" light. Many public companies have been faced with this situation when their administrators were charged with financial malfeasance, processes were shown to be environmentally irresponsible or promotions suspected of deliberately violating "truth in advertising" laws, for example. Following is a scenario in which you must publicly address a situation that has the potential to impact relationships with one or more of your organization's key publics.

Important Background Information:

HealthWay Pharmacies, Inc. prides itself on its commitment to the community and its high standards for quality control in its prescription handling, billing and financial accounting, and record-keeping. As a result, it has come to enjoy a high level of loyalty from the YourState community, even as high profile, national pharmacies have tried to establish a foothold in the region.

Plans are in place to expand the HealthWay retail services to NextState and to vastly increase its market share in the prescription by mail industry. The advertising and public relations campaigns are being planned around the theme "Your Health is our Way". The HealthWay sales department is recruiting satisfied customers to provide testimonials for the ads.

The Situation:

You have just received a call from the health editor of the Anytown newspaper saying it has information that HealthWay has been accused of releasing information about patients to other patients in its Mail-Meds service. This violates federal privacy regulations as well as the HealthWay commitment to its clients and its customers.

The editor will not reveal the source of his information, but you have reason to believe it may be Gina Mathison, a former HealthWay customer service supervisor who is now working for a competitor that is already established in the NextState market and that may be a rival for the NextState mail prescription contract. Mathison was terminated six months ago for falsifying expense reports.

The newspaper editor has assigned a reporter to follow up on the charges and determine if they are true and if it is indeed a story. The reporter intends to file the story with or without HealthWay comment as part of an ongoing series on the dangers of modern medicine. Your inquiries show that the story may be true with regard to two situations with which Mathison was in close contact. In both cases Mail-Meds patients reported receiving vials of prescriptions with two prescription labels, one correct for that patient and a second exactly underneath for another patient. These labels include the patient's name, physician's name, name of medication, dosage and instructions for administering the medication. The patients discovered the error when they peeled their own label off for privacy reasons before destroying the vial. They notified HealthWay of the error and questioned the company's privacy controls and its policy regarding the recycling of containers.

Matheson's customer service team investigated the charges and identified a misperforming labelling machine as the source of the problem. Several other vials with a similar but less precise placement of the top label had been caught at the quality control stage. In all cases the medication in the vial was the medication for the patient who received it. The fact remains that at least the two vials in question escaped the eye of the quality control team.

HealthWay purchases new containers for all prescription products, and believes there is no way that a recycled container could have been used.

Persuasive Messages
Background to Exercises 14-2, 14-3 and 14-4

This background information will be used for three assignments in Chapter Fourteen. Following is a scenario in which HealthWay might feel compelled to issue a persuasive message. Note that ValleyLINK Communications, another of the text clients, will be writing in opposition to propose that funds that threaten its programs should be restored.

For the "Letter to the Editor" assignment you should assume that the Anytown newspaper has printed an editorial supporting the retention of funds for education, including educational technology.

The Situation:

The economic crisis in YourState has not abated, and Governor _____ continues to make cuts in programs that were initiated by his predecessor in office, a governor from the opposite party. Two such programs are the prescription subsidies for the retired members of the YourState State Employees Association (YSEA) and for the children of families below the poverty level.

The loss of these programs will have a serious impact on HealthWay's Mail-Meds program. 35% of the YSEA subscribers were retirees taking advantage of the subsidy. Some of HealthWay's urban retail stores receive up to 40% of their prescription business from families recieving the child health subsidy.

You have been working with the team that is developing the organization's response to this threat. Among other tactics, you have recommended that HealthWay should make a greater effort to persuade the Anytown legislative representatives to vote against cutting the subsidies and to carry your message to the governor and state legislature.

You have recommended a two-pronged strategy: contacting the legislators directly; and persuading the Anytown community to add its voice to your cause. The HealthWay president has directed you to draft the first letters in this campaign. *Note: You are free to determine some details of the effects of the cuts, but do not assume that the programs are in danger of closing down.*

Conferences and Trade Fairs
Background to Exercise 16-8

In anticipation of its expansion into NextState, HealthWay has decided to participate in the annual "Community Health Conference and Fair" sponsored by the NextState Department of Health. The one-day conference will bring together business, civic and social services leaders to discuss how they can raise awareness of the programs and services available to help NextState residents to improve and maintain their health.

Conference Details: Dates: ....Friday Oct. 17 (4–8 p.m.) and Saturday Oct, 18 (9 a.m.–8 p.m.)

Location: ....Civic Center, Capitalcity, NS

Theme: ....The theme for the fair will be ""Health for All"

Display Details: Booths: ....8' x 8' spaces, Booth #34 will be reserved as the conference information booth.

Continued

Standard : ....Each booth will include one 3' x 6' table with gray skirt plus gray backdrop, three electric outlets.

Extras available: ..Television and video monitors, VCRs at additional cost.

Food Service: ......Coffee, tea, soft drinks and sandwiches will be available at designated locations throughout the fair.

Program: ....Conference organizers produce a program that includes a listing of the names and addresses of all vendors. They will also accept ads for this program.

Vendor Schedule: The official drawing for any prizes offered by individual vendors will be held at the information booth at 6 p.m. on Saturday evening.

Media Coverage: _____ TV Channel #__ will broadcast live throughout the Friday and Saturday evening news shows. Typically they feature live action with vendors that have activities or interesting give-aways, especially for children. The NextState City newspaper will also likely send a reporter and photographer as soon as the Fair opens on Friday for the Saturday edition.

The NextState City newspaper annual health supplement is published two weeks before the Fair, and advertising space is available.

Vendor Schedule: The official drawing for any prizes offered by individual vendors will be held at the Chamber of Commerce booth at noon on Friday.

ValleyLINK Focus: HealthWay will feature the "Mail-Meds" program at its booth, focusing on the cost and convenience benefits to families and senior citizens. HealthWay has produced a five minute video about the program.

You may be able to use the brochure you created in Exercise 15-3 if it is compatible with your exhibit theme.

From the desk of
Lou Anderson

Dear _____:

Welcome to ValleyLINK Communications! It is good to have you on our team and I hope you enjoy working with us.

We know that joining a new company is always a learning process so we will be assigning you a corporate mentor for the next few months. Your mentor will be able to answer questions about your job, your benefits, our social activities, and the company as a whole. And don't hesitate to ask help from anyone on the staff. I think you will find we are a friendly group and that, time permitting, we will all be willing to help you find your niche on our team.

Please read the enclosed brief policy manual as soon as possible. It covers all of the legal and benefits information you must know about the company as well as introducing you to the policies that help us maintain a true team approach, even as we grow.

You will soon learn that we all work very hard: when deadlines approach we all pitch in to help; and when rewards are earned, everyone gets to share in them. We are pleased that you have joined our team. We look forward to hearing your ideas and to working with you. We hope you enjoy your career with our company. And please feel free to stop in my office any time the door is open.

Lou Anderson
President

PROFILE: Goals:

ValleyLINK goals: Current Year

Increase revenues by 40 percent

- *Sign 2,700 new household clients*
- *Sign 55 new business clients*

Expand services to entire YourState

- *Support links to North Region and West Region*
- *Establish regular presence in local media*

Act on commitment to community service

- *Add four school districts to "Edu-Link" program*
- *Develop programs to support "Edu-link" program*

Expand training for clients

- *Develop user-friendly, e-mail training package*

Staff Expansion/Development

- *Hire 12 new technical specialists and four additional customer service reps to maintain customer service in expanding subscriber base.*
- *Hire community development specialist to develop the use of the Internet in the programs of Valley government, education and health organizations*
- *Introduce 401K plan, initially without employer contributions*
- *Join local credit bureau*

PROFILE: ValleyLINK people: who's who and where they work...

	President	**Legal Counsel**
	Lou Anderson	

Dir. Administration		**Dir. Tech Services**		**Dir. Sales and Mktng**	
Lyn Smith		Pete Hamilton		Alex Hale	
HR and Admin	Accounting	Tech Devel.	Tech Services	Marketing	Sales
Joan Marshall	Mike Carson	Kevin Aston	Wally Warner	Jean Samuels	Will Tyson
Human Res.	Payroll	Research/Dev.	Installation	Training	Sales Reps.
Purchasing	Billing	Software Dev.		Client Education	Client Serv. Reps
Office Mgmnt	Collections			Tech Writing	Sales Clerical
				Public Relations	
				Communications	
				Desktop Design	

PROFILE: How we earn our living . . .

Services:

ValleyLINK Communications offers a full-service Internet access program to all subscribers. This service includes:

High-Quality Speed and Service:

- Duplicate T-1 lines to different Internet companies for high-speed, reliable service; our router determines the fastest route for data, even if one provider is "down" or overloaded;
- Support for super-fast, digital ISDN technology;
- Dial in access compatible with 14.4, 19.2, 28.8 or 56 K modems.

Access Options:

- Unlimited access to Internet newsgroups, "chat rooms," and bulletin boards;
- Unlimited Web browsing, through any browser;
- Access to many standard search engines and directories, including AltaVista, Google, Webcrawl, Search.com, Yahoo, Lycos, and Excite;
- Personal dial-up accounts for electronic mail storage or mail forwarding.

Customer Services

- 24-hour on-line and telephone "Help Desk";
- Personalized training for all subscribers;
- Quarterly newsletters to introduce new services, answer often-asked questions and help users maximize the benefits of our programs and services.

Web site Design and Maintenance:

- Web site design;
- Web site hosting with unlimited access;
- Domain-name searches, mapping and maintenance.

Security:

- Firewall;
- Secure web server including password access and data encryption for secure data transfer;
- Web-filtering software available on-line for managing personal access to the web.

Optional Services:

- Additional hard disk space available;
- Data back-up services.

PROFILE: _More about our business and our company......._

Products:

ValleyLINK offers three Internet services, each one tailored specifically to the needs of a particular user-audience:

■   "PersonaLINK" — a cost-effective, user-friendly program aimed at households and other individual users. It features individualized training, a 24-hour dial-in or telephone "Help-Desk" and optional downloadable web-filtering software.

■   "CommerciaLINK" — the fastest, most reliable service available to Central Valley business for Internet access and efficient, cost-effective data transfer with a level of access and data security most businesses cannot afford to implement themselves. Full-time training and customer service representatives support each CommerciaLINK account.

■   "EduLINK" — our newest service, providing Central Valley schools with inexpensive Internet access and in-school networking.

Media Releases Issued This Year:

"_____ _(name of nearby town)_ joins the Net"

"_____ _(name of nearby town)_ joins the Net"

"Education and the Internet" an interview with Lou Anderson _(in the Anytown Schools Parent's Newsletter)_

"Service is the Key Part of ISP" in _____ _(name of town - sent to local business magazine)_

"The Internet in Your Future" in the Anytown newspaper Sunday Lifestyle Section.
Reprinted in _____ _(local magazine.)_

PROFILE: *A short history of ValleyLINK;*
That's all there is......

5 years ago:

January	Office opened in Anytown, YourState
	Staff: Lou Anderson, Pete Hamilton and Alex Hale
	Service region: Anytown local region
February	Signed first client
August	Employed two technical development specialists
	Employed first customer service rep for after-hours "Help Desk" :
	now available 8 am - midnight (M-F) and 8 am - 6 pm (Sat./Sun.)
October	Written up in _____ *(local business magazine)*
End Year 1........	3,246 clients, 10 staff, $987,802 annual sales

3 years ago:

March	Increased service area to include _____ *(name towns)*
May	Published first issue of our client newsletter, the *ValleyLinkage*
July	Increased service area to include _____ *(name towns)*
August	Launched "EduLINK" program
	Selected as internet provider for 4 school districts: _____ *(name)*
October	Joined Anytown Chamber of Commerce
	Moved office to larger premises in _____ YourState
End Year 3........	11,167 clients, 31 staff, $3,500,000 annual sales

Last year:

January	Employed full-time technical writer
February	Increased service area to include _____ *(name towns)*
March	Selected as internet provider for Anytown Health System
May	Received internet contract for _____Schools
July	Received internet contract for YourState Power Company
September........	Staff reached 50
	Expanded "Help-Desk" hours to 6 a.m.–midnight, 7 days a week
November	Employed tenth internal customer service rep. for "Help-desk"
End Year 5........	23,220 clients, 56 staff, $5,102,333 million annual sales

This year:

February	Named one of "Top Ten Fastest growing companies" by the
	Anytown Chamber of Commerce

PROFILE: _Money-matters..._
Web sites you'll find useful...

Financial data and growth statistics:

	This Year	Last Year
INCOME		
Fees from subscribers	$3,500,000	$2,700,000
Fees from hosting web site	1,250,000	700,000
Consulting fees: design and networking	250,000	100,000
Total Income	$5,000,000	$3,500,000
EXPENSES		
Staff (salaries, commissions, insurance)	3,200,000	2,600,000
Facilities (rent, insurance, maintenance)	800,000	400,000
Computer costs	500,000	300,000
Advertising and promotion	75,000	60,000
Interest on long-term debt	200,000	25,000
Other	25,000	15,000
Total expenses	$4,800,000	$3,400,000
OPERATING PROFIT	**$200,000**	**$100,000**

# Subscribers	Commercial Web sites Hosted
4 years ago 3,500	60
2 years ago 14,000	400
Last Year 27,800	600
This Year 36,200	850

Web sites to get you started:

CINet Guide to Internet Service Providers: ....<www.cnet.com>
   You can search national ISPs, by area(s) served, or alphabetically

Berkeley Software Design, Inc., "Becoming an ISP": ....<www.bdsi.com/info/becoming>

Choosing an Internet Service Provicer:.........http://www.microsoft.com/athome/security/connect/isp.mspx

Information on Aging and Mental Health

Department of Health and Human Services: ....<www.hhs.gov>

JAMA, The Journal of the American Medical Association:......<www.ama-assn.org/public/journals/jama>

New England Journal of Medicine: ....<www.nejm.org/content/index.asp>
                                             (full text for subscribers only)

PROFILE: Policies and other things you need to know....

Office Hours:

The ValleyLINK office is open Monday - Friday from 6 am to 10 pm and from 6 am to 4 pm on Saturdays.

All employees are paid for a 40-hour work week. However, because we believe that our staff are paid to do a job rather than punch a clock, you may set your own work schedule subject to the following guidelines:

- All schedules must be at least 40 hours and are subject to the approval of your supervisor. Approval will be based on the need to maintain appropriate staffing levels in every department at all times and to ensure that all responsibilities are covered. For example, the customer service department must be staffed at all times that the office is open.

- All staff must be available for a weekly department meeting. Your supervisor will advise the time of your department meeting.

- All managers must be available for a weekly managers' meeting currently scheduled at 1:30 pm. every Monday.

- You must take at least a half-hour unpaid "lunch" break during each workday to give yourself a chance to relax and get a fresh perspective.

Personal Space:

We recognize that different employees work best in different environments.

Employees with offices and/or cubicles may have personal music systems -- radios, tape or CD players -- as long as you play them with headphones. The music must not be audible to anyone else in the office. Be aware that excessive "air guitar" playing will be regarded as not working and you may be asked to disband your group.

ValleyLINK is not responsible for the safety or security of any personal equipment you may bring to the office.

Employees may display a limited number of photos, posters or art works in the immediate vicinity of their desk, although we ask you to remember that this is a public space and that everyone's taste in the visual arts is not the same.

Break Room:

In our break room we provide unlimited coffee, juice and bottled water for all staff. This will continue unless we perceive that this privilege is being abused.

Staff may also keep their own food and beverages in the refrigerator and heat food in the microwave. All dirty dishes should be put in the dishwasher before 5 pm each day. Our cleaners will wash them each evening and put the cleaned dishes on the counter.

Background to Writing Assignments: ValleyLINK

Following is background information you will need for some of the writing exercises in this workbook. Instructions for the exercises can be found in Part Two of the workbook.

Organizational Culture

Background to Exercise 4-2

Following is the text of a conversation between the ValleyLINK president and director of administration regarding the need for a dress code. It tells you what is behind the code and the limits the company wants.

Lyn: "Lou, I know you don't want to hear this, but Joan Marshall and I think we need to consider a dress code."

Lou: "Dress code! One of the reasons I started my own company was so nobody would tell me what to wear . . ."

Lyn: "I agree in principle, but I'm concerned we could be letting ourselves in for trouble if we don't put some standards in place. I mean, how about the messages I've been seeing on t-shirts around the office? Right now I think they're mostly funny, but some of them are getting pretty tasteless. And the way Joe and Luke carry on when Luke wears his "Tigers Rule!" baseball cap, it's a wonder either of them get anything done.

"We're looking to double our staff in the next six months and I'm afraid it will get out of control. All it will take is one offended staff member and we could have a lawsuit on our hands. Look what happened to the guy who discussed the Seinfeld episode at the water cooler. It cost his employer millions and the guy wasn't even wearing the offensive words."

Lou: "I hate to admit it, but you may be right. It made me feel old, but even I got turned off when the kid with the "Sex, booze and a bong" t-shirt and the Yankees cap on backward came for an interview last week. It actually crossed my mind that if he couldn't even pay more attention to how he looked for a job interview, how could we expect him to take care with his work, much less our image.

"Okay, I'll look at a dress code; just don't touch jeans, okay? I've got a whole closet full of 'em."

Lyn: "Right, and you also know enough to put on a suit when you meet with the bankers."

Lou: "It's a sports jacket....but still, no ties. No one should ever be forced to wear a tie."

Lyn: "Okay, I'll get PR to draft it up and we'll fly it past you next week. That will give us time to get it ironed out before we start recruiting again in six weeks."

News writing

Background to Exercise 9-4

Following are a series of conversations leading up to a decision by the ValleyLINK management to launch a new service: "SeniorLINK".

<u>Conversation overheard in coffee room</u>

Joe: *"Whew! What a weekend. I planned to reconcile my checkbook, but my son taught his grandfather to play computer chess and all of a sudden I couldn't get near the machine. They were having a great time. This is the same grandfather who always says, 'if the Almighty had intended me to use a computer, he'd have made my hand a little rat or hamster or whatever you call that thing'."*

<u>At a management meeting later that week</u>

Lou: "I overheard Joe Stevens telling how his son taught his grandfather to play computer chess and I got to thinking that we might be able to use that idea. We always talk about some sort of community service, and I think promoting computer use for senior citizens might be worthwhile. We could set up stations at senior centers and teach them to send e-mail messages to their families. That would be a cost-savings for them so they might get interested. And it's fairly easy to learn . . ."

Joan: *"....Maybe some teacher would be willing to link her class with a senior center. That might be good for the seniors and the kids. My sister-in-law is PTO president at Claremont Elementary and she probably knows the computer teacher there...."*

Mike: "Sure, we can absorb the installation and monthly charges, but there's also the computers and printers for each of the sites, and we'll have to pay someone to set up the web site and accounts and teach the seniors to use it all....."

Joan: *"Well, there may still be some funding available from the county Department of the Aging, but I'm not sure when the applications were due. And I think there is probably some private foundation money out there for projects like these. The hospital can probably help us with that as part of their mental health program. Don't we have some contacts there?"*

"How about the interns? Would the college approve their doing the web site or set-ups or teaching as part of their internships? That would help us hold costs."

Pete: "I can have Phil Alley check into that. I can't see a problem."

Mike: *"Yeah, but it's still going to take time on our part. Who's going to coordinate it from here and how are we going to pay for it?"*

Lou: "Okay, that's enough, we've got all the issues on the table. Let's do our homework and see if this is feasible. Pete, Joan, Mike, can you check with your contacts and see what we can do. We can start on a small scale just to see if it can work. And Mike, do a quick trial budget to see what is possible. Let's all report back at the next meeting."

<u>Continued</u>

<u>Four months later</u>

1. Funding from the counties has already been allocated for this year. Applications for the next year are due four months from now, with approval in eight months.

2. The Director of Community Affairs at the Anytown Health Community Relations Office volunteered one or two of the Anytown Health senior centers as a trial site. She has agreed to make space available and provide a computer and printer at each center chosen. The only condition is that the project must help seniors get involved and communicate with the outside world, which she believes will help promote a positive mental attitude. There are studies to support this. (*HINT: we have provided the web site addresses for the Journal of the American Medical Association and the Department of Health and Human Services*).

3. National Mental Health Week is in six weeks. What influence could this have on your release?

4. The Senior Centers Coalition will be happy to participate in the program. You can use any of their twelve centers.

5. Educational information:
   * The YourState fifth grade curriculum focuses on the student's own town.
   * Junior high English classes do a project writing real-life stories.
   * By the fifth grade, all students are expected to know simple word processing.

6. The Central College Computer Department has approved using students to design the web site for the senior centers, set up the accounts and develop new programs. Phil is now talking with the college to see if students can use tutoring at the senior centers to fill their Community Service requirement. It looks like a go but it won't happen until next year.

7. Luke Olson's wife works at HealthWay Pharmacies, Inc., which is replacing all of the PCs in their Anytown office. The HealthWay board agreed to donate one machine and a small laser printer for this project. All you have to do is pick it up.

8. Good News! The Foundation for Senior Action (FSA) has approved a $30,000 grant to support a one-year trial of the program provided it is launched in at least six senior centers in the first six months. This will pay for an assistant for Jeanie Samuels so she can oversee the project and act as liaison with the senior centers. Part of the assistant's job will be to act as trainer/consultant.

Feature writing

Background to Exercise 10-2

Following is the raw material for a feature story that the management of ValleyLINK wants to use in its annual report to subscribers. Management believes this article will add some "human interest" to what is often perceived as a cold, technology-based industry while also demonstrating the company's expertise and concern for the community.

The basis of the story is the "SeniorLINK" project which [for the purpose of this assignment is at the end of its first complete year] and on which you previously wrote a news release in Exercise 9-4. The information below has been selected to give you a wide range of options for writing the feature story.

Highlights of the first year of "SeniorLINK"

- Senior Link began operations 12 months ago at the AnytownSenior Center run by Anytown Health System. Additional centers were opened at Othertown (10 months ago) and Sometown (9 months ago) senior centers and at several Senior Centers Coalition sites (seven months ago).

■ Senior citizens who signed up for the program and attended a training session were given a personal e-mail address on a special ValleyLINK site: <name@valleylinkseniors.xxx>

■ For the first six months, training needs were met by volunteers from ValleyLINK, but during the most recent school term, five computer students from Central Valley College supplemented the ValleyLINK efforts.

■ In September, six senior citizens from the Anytown Senior Center agreed to work with Elise Johnson's fifth grade class from the Elms Elementary School on a three-month project to write a history of Anytown in the 20th century. All of the seniors had grown up in the area and the family of one octogenarian had farmed in the region for over 200 years.

Students researched the village history (records of which stopped at 1900) in the library and then used e-mail to ask questions of their senior sources, who also answered on-line. At the end of the project the class visited the senior center and presented each of their sources with a hand-illustrated copy of the history the students had written.

■ In February, the Anytown Senior Center solicited volunteers to work with eighth graders in schools serviced by Valley Link on their life-story writing projects. Twenty seniors volunteered. The students interviewed their subjects "on-line" first to identify an event in the senior's life to write about and then to obtain details for the story.

English teacher _____ submitted the story written by _____ about how senior citizen Pete Callahan got his nickname "Cowboy Callahan" to a state-wide junior high short story contest. The story won second place and Mr. Callahan was able to attend the award presentation _____. *(You may provide details.)*

■ Sign-in sheets and log-on records for the year show that 247 seniors have logged onto the system since the start of the program. Over 70 percent of these sign-ons have occurred in the last four months.

■ Anytown Health System has provided three additional terminals for each of their senior centers as demand increased. The other sites have had to limit usage to 20 minutes per log-on during peak usage hours and have requested additional terminals.

Because ValleyLINK met the condition of The Foundation for Senior Action to open six sites within six months (See News Writing Assignment) the Foundation has agreed to provide an additional $15,000 which will be used to purchase and install the additional terminals.

Spokespersons

The following people could be expected to be the subject of this article and/or comment for this article, depending on the topic and theme you choose to pursue. It is your responsibility to select the appropriate spokespersons and to write any quotes from them. Next to each person we have identified the attitude this person would likely have toward the project. This attitude should be reflected in his or her words.

Except for the ValleyLINK personnel and the mayor (whom you have previously identified), you may name any of the people. You may assume that anyone in an official capacity has agreed that his or her name may be used, but it is possible some of the private citizens may not wish to be named. How can you deal with this?

Possible spokespersons	Attitude, likely message
* ValleyLINK president and program head	Positive; credit staff, community; aware of PR opportunity, mission-driven
* Anytown Mayor	Enthusiastic; political; take some credit
* Principals of schools involved	Positive; mission-driven
* Directors of senior centers involved	Enthusiastic, positive, forward-looking
* Senior and student participants	Willing to tell their stories, enthusiastic

Newsletters

Background to Exercises 10-4 and 10-5

You are responsible for compiling newsletters for company staff and clients. The following stories are the raw material for both newsletters — the first issues in the new calendar year. Some of the items will go in both issues, others only in one or neither. Completing the exercise in the text for this assignment will help you determine which articles to include in each document. Be aware that these items are presented "as you received them." Putting them in grammatical or consistent style is your job.

- <u>Dress code:</u> It has been approved as you wrote it. _(Note: The HR Director is concerned staff may not take this seriously and that work time will be lost while they complain about it). What tone should you take? Why?_

- <u>President's Message:</u> He wants a draft of a topical article for this month.

- <u>SeniorLINK launch:</u> The news story you wrote in Exercise 9-4 will be the basis for the lead news story for the newsletters. Exercise 10-5 will guide you through adapting this story to newsletter style.

- <u>Chamber of Commerce:</u> Alex Hale has been elected second vice president of the Anytown Chamber of Commerce. He will be responsible for membership and elections. In two years, he will succeed to the presidency.

- <u>Technical Development:</u> The hardware is here for the new "firewall". It will be installed by the beginning of next month and will provide another level of security for all users. We expect our CommerciaLINK customers to be especially pleased.

- <u>Births:</u> . . . . _Following is a notice you saw on the bulletin board in the coffee room: "_____'s girlfriend _____ had a baby boy — 9lbs, 4 oz. Hope he doesn't look like his dad."_

- <u>Engagements:</u> _Following is a phone message from "Sandy": "_____ got engaged. The ring is huge! Can it go in the newsletter?"_

- <u>Accounting News:</u> We will have W-2 tax forms out to all employees by the end of the month. If you have any questions refer them to _____ at extension 100.

- <u>Illness:</u> _____'s father is recovering from surgery. _____'s son broke his leg playing soccer.

- <u>Long Service:</u> _Following is a memo from HR._ "The following long service awards were presented at the holiday party. Please feature in next newsletter." _(You may name)._

- <u>Credit Bureau:</u> Joan Marshall says the company has finalized arrangements to join the YourState and Purchasing Bureau. Staff will be able to use this for a range of financial services and discount purchasing at stores throughout the region A bureau representative will be here early next month to explain the program and sign up new members. You must be a full-time ValleyLINK staff member for at least one year in order to be eligible. After the first sign-up, new member sign-ups will be held twice each year. We hope staff will find this service useful.

- <u>Softball Sign-Ups:</u> Jean Samuels wants us to field a team in the Anytown corporate slow-pitch softball league-amateur division, this summer. Games are Mondays and Wednesdays June 1 - July 15. Teams are 10-members each (including four outfielders) and we must have equal numbers of men and women on the field and in the line-up at all times. If we can get commitments from 15 staff/spouses/friends etc. before the first of next month, the company will pay the entry fee and provide t-shirts.

- Cartoon: _____ left you the following note scrawled on a memo pad: "Found this cartoon in my file the other day. Hope it is clear enough for you to use."

  Note: the cartoon is very clear.

- New Employees: _____ - Technical Development Specialist, previously worked as a consultant in the Academic Computing Department at Central College.

- Sales News: The following was provided by the Sales Director. *(Hint: Except in very special circumstances, ValleyLINK management does not makes its client list or marketing plans public. Why do you think this is the case? Think about how pleased your sales reps would be to know the client list of your competitors.)*

  "PersonaLINK" sales reps signed 14 new households in November and December, most of them from our booth during the "Support Valley Businesses" festival at the Claremont Mall. (I think this is a record). _____ is trying to get a list of graduating seniors from the local colleges to offer them a special deal on individual accounts during May and June. After months of negotiations, _____ swears he's going to sign Anytown Medical Center to a "CommerciaLINK" contract this month. All sales staff will be at the Chamber of Conference business fair in March.

- Tech Writers: *Following is a plea from _____:* "Please, please, please, would everyone pay more attention to the deadlines for copy for sales proposals. These are time-sensitive and the other writers need time to put all the drafts together into one final document. The Sales Department says there are three big RFPs (Requests for Proposal) coming in the next few months so we are going to have our hands full. Please, when we ask you for copy, have it in on time. If you can't, please talk to me as soon as you receive the assignment.

- Suggestions: The following was found in the Suggestion Box during the last month.

  "I think we should have a special recognition for the Employee of the Month . How about reserving the parking spot closest to the door for that person for a month."

Crisis Writing

Background to Exercises 12-1, 12-2 and 12-3

Sometimes it is necessary to publicly address issues that may embarrass or otherwise show your client in a "less than favorable" light. Many public companies have been faced with this situation when their administrators were charged with financial malfeasance, processes were shown to be environmentally irresponsible or promotions suspected of deliberately violating "truth in advertising" laws, for example. Following is a scenario in which you must publicly address a situation that has the potential to impact relationships with one or more of your organization's key publics.

Important Background Information:

ValleyLINK has always prided itself on the loyalty it has enjoyed from the Anytown community, even as large service providers have tried to establish a foothold in the region. In particular, subscribers to the ValleyLINK CommerciaLINK service have doubled over the last five years with ValleyLINK now holding an estimated 65% of the market. The rest is shared over several companies. These subscribers include the Anytown city government and its agencies, including the school department.

Plans are in place to expand the CommerciaLINK service to the rest of YourState, with PersonaLINK Services to follow. The advertising and public relations campaigns are being planned around the theme "Now _____ (name of town) can enjoy the best". The ValleyLINK sales department is recruiting Anytown businesses and city agencies (which also use the service) to provide testimonials for the ads.

The Situation:

You have just received a call from the business editor of the Anytown newspaper saying it has information that ValleyLINK has provided kickbacks for the last three years to the Anytown mayor and four city councillors in return for their support in ValleyLINK's selection as preferred vendor for the city government and its agencies.

The editor will not reveal the source of his information, but you have reason to believe it may be Gerald Mathison, a former ValleyLINK sales manager who is now working for a competitor that you believe wants to enter the Anytown market. Mathison was terminated six months ago for falsifying expense reports. He was on the sales team that developed the proposal for the Anytown government contract and was sales representative and liaison to many of the agencies that used the service.

The newspaper editor has assigned a reporter to follow up on the charges and determine if they are true and if it is indeed, a story. The reporter intends to file the story with or without ValleyLINK comment. Your inquiries show that the story may be true with regard to two state or city agencies with which Mathison was in close contact. *(You may name them)*. In both cases the agency contracting officers with which Mathison worked have since left the agencies and the area. It appears that any misconduct, if such existed, was between Mathison and these two officers and that the payoffs may have been part of the falsified expense reports.

ValleyLINK management learned of the charges at the same time as the newspaper, from new procurement officers inside the agencies. They are both about to announce that they will reopen the bidding process for the ISP contract. ValleyLINK may submit a proposal.

Persuasive Messages
Background to Exercises 14-2, 14-3, and 14-4

This background information will be used for two assignments in Chapter Fourteen. Following is a scenario in which ValleyLINK might feel compelled to issue a persuasive message. Note that HealthWay Pharmacies, another of the text clients, will be writing in opposition to propose that funds that threaten its programs should be restored.

For the "Letter to the Editor" assignment you should assume that the Anytown newspaper has printed an editorial supporting the retention of funds for medical subsidies for the elderly and children of families below the poverty level.

The Situation:

The economic crisis in YourState has not abated, and Governor _____ continues to make cuts in programs that were initiated by his predecessor in office, a governor from the opposing party. One such program is the YourState Electronic Information Program which provides subsidies and low interest loans to educational institutions and non-profit organizations to create web sites and develop computer training for their students and members.

The loss of this program will have a serious impact on ValleyLINK's EduLINK and SeniorLINK programs.

You have been working with the team that is developing the organization's response to this threat. Among other tactics, you have recommended that ValleyLINK should make a greater effort to persuade the Anytown legislative representatives to vote against cutting the YourState Electronic Information Program and to carry your message to the governor and state legislature.

You have recommended a two-pronged strategy: contacting the legislators directly; and persuading the Anytown community to add its voice to your cause. The ValleyLINK president has directed you to draft the first letters in this campaign. *Note: You are free to determine some details of the effects of the cuts, but do not assume that the programs are in danger of closing based on current projections.*

Conferences and Trade Fairs

Background to Exercise 16-8

ValleyLINK has been invited to participate in the annual "Community Awareness Conference and Fair" sponsored by the Anytown Mayor's Office and Chamber of Commerce. The one-day conference will bring together community business, civic and social services leaders to discuss how they can raise community awareness of the needs and services available to disadvantaged populations in the community.

Conference Details:	Dates: ....Friday Oct. 17 (4–8 p.m.) and Saturday Oct, 18 (9 a.m.–8 p.m.)	
	Location: ....Anytown Civic Center, Anytown, YS	
	Theme: ....The theme for the fair will be "Get Involved"	
Display Details:	Booths: ....8' x 8' spaces, Booth #34 will be reserved as the conference information booth.	
	Standard : ....Each booth will include one 3' x 6' table with gray skirt plus gray backdrop, three electric outlets.	
	Extras available: ..Television and video monitors, VCRs at additional cost	
	Food Service: ......Coffee, tea, soft drinks and sandwiches will be available at designated locations throughout the fair.	
	Program: ....Conference organizers produce a program that includes a listing of the names and addresses of all vendors. They will also accept ads for this program.	
Vendor Schedule:	The official drawing for any prizes offered by individual vendors will be held at the information booth at 6 p.m. on Saturday evening.	
Media Coverage:	_____ TV Channel #__ will broadcast live throughout the Friday and Saturday evening news shows. Typically they feature live action with vendors that have activities or interesting giveaways, especially for children. The Anytown newspaper will also likely send a reporter and photographer as soon as the Fair opens on Friday for the Saturday edition.	
	The Anytown newspaper annual "A Focus on Our Community" supplement is published in September, two weeks before the Fair, and advertising space is available.	
Vendor Schedule:	The official drawing for any prizes offered by individual vendors will be held at the Chamber of Commerce booth at noon on Friday.	
ValleyLINK Focus:	ValleyLINK will feature the "SeniorLINK" program at its booth, focusing on the mental health benefits to the involved senior citizens. ValleyLINK has produced a five minute video of seniors and their student partners discussing the program and can likely get several senior-student pairs to engage in interactive computer activities at the booth.	
	You may be able to use the brochure you created in Exercise 15-3 if it is compatible with your exhibit theme.	

Getting Started

This project will help you understand the environment in which your client operates. It will also help you identify the publics who may be important to that organization, where to find them, and how to reach them.

The rest of your projects will be based on the answers you find for this research.

Resources: The following resources will help you answer the questions on this worksheet.

- The U.S. Census: www.census.gov
- The website: www.epodunk.com

  From the home page, select your state and type in the town or city you want. If the location is among the more than 2,500 in the epodunk database you will get a city profile, plus links to relevant census data, and to government, business, and organizational information.

- Websites for the cities and towns in the region you have selected. Many of these are linked from the epodunk.com source.

- The population profiles available through the Prizm® system at www.claritas.com. From the home page select "You are where you live." You will be able to select the segmentation program you want to use (please use either Prizm or Prizm NE) and type in the zip code. The program will immediately give you the five most prominent population segments in that zip code.

- Local business directories and phone books
- Google searches – be creative

Define your client:

1. Who is your client?

2. Describe your client's "business" as you understand it.

3. Describe your relationship with this client. What will your client want you to do?

Defining the region in which your client operates

In this section, you will begin to develop a profile of the region in which your client operates so you know the resources you will have available for reaching your client's many publics.

1.   Identify the main population centers in your client's region. Your client will provide services in and gain support from one or more of these centers.

_____   _____

_____   _____

_____   _____

_____   _____

2.   List below the local and regional media that service your client's region

Daily press: _____   Other press: _____

_____   _____

_____   _____

_____   _____

_____   _____

Magazines/specialty publications: _____   _____

_____   _____

_____   _____

_____   _____

Radio stations call letters/name: _____   Characterize the station (e.g., teen, talk),

_____   _____

_____   _____

_____   _____

_____   _____

_____   _____

_____   _____

_____   _____

<u>TV stations (other than cable channels)</u> _____   <u>Total local news/programming time</u> _____

_____   _____

_____   _____

_____   _____

3. Identify at least five (5) businesses that operate in your client's area. If your client is a business, try to identify businesses that would compete for customers with your client. If your client is a non-profit organization, try to identify businesses that you might tap for support because they share a location, clientele, or goal with your organization.

_____   _____

_____   _____

_____   _____

_____   _____

_____   _____

_____   _____

4. Identify at least five (5) non-profic, social and/or civic organizations that operate in your client's region. If your client is a business, try to identify organizations with which you have something in common, such as location, goal, etc. These are organizations that you might consider supporting. If your client is a non-profit organization, try to identify organizations which will compete with your client for donations as well as organizations with which your client might team up.

_____   _____

_____   _____

_____   _____

_____   _____

_____   _____

5. Identify the political figures who might be instrumental in affecting your client, through local support or legislation. You may have to advocate with them on behalf of your client. You should be able to identify at least two appropriate names in each category.

<u>Category</u> <u>Name</u>   <u>Party/district served</u>

U.<u>S. Senator(s)</u>   _____

_____

US Congressional
Representatives
from the area

_____

_____

_____

_____

_____

State Senator(s)

_____

_____

_____

State Representative(s)

_____

_____

_____

_____

_____

Mayor(s):

_____

_____

_____

_____

Other prominent
public figures
(that you might use for
support or as spokes-
persons, for example)

_____

_____

_____

_____

Define your client's publics

1.   Begin to develop a profile of the publics your client will want to reach with a public relations campaign. On the "Publics Profile" form, identify *at least* ten (10) publics with which your client might have a relationship that may require public relations activity. The publics must differ in the relationship your client wants to have with them (i.e., the purpose of your communica-

tion), the attitude, knowledge or involvement they have toward or with your client (i.e., that will affect the messages you send) and/or the ways you will likely reach them (i.e., the media you will use). Consider especially publics that relate to the needs your client has for your services.

2.   For each public identify on the "Publics Profile" what your client wants from the public or what your client hopes to achieve as the result of your public relations efforts. Why is your client interested in conducting a public relations campaign with this public?

3.   Next run a Claritas search to help identify where these publics may be located and what characteristics they may have. It may help you to start by listing ten zip codes in the region in which your client operates. This is why we wanted you to define an actual region.

       Using the Claritas "You are where you live" segmentation system on www.claritas.com try to identify where you will find your organization's publics in these zip codes and enter the zip code and city name in the appropriate space on the "Publics Profile." When you type in a zip code, the program will give you the five most prominent segments in that zip code. Clicking on the segment name will produce a brief description of that segment, including income level, general population description and some basic likes/dislikes or lifestyle facts. From this information you should be able to make some generalizations about whether any of the publics are likely to be located in that zip code, as well as about the message themes and media you might use to reach them.

       NOTE: You may not be able to use all of the zip codes. Similarly, you may not be able to identify a zip code for many of your publics. You should, however, be able to identify at least the zip codes of publics who would use your client's services and who would contribute to your client's success. You may also get clues regarding the interests and preferences of people who fit the profile of some publics.

4.   Finally, identify at least five (5) ways that you believe you could effectively reach each public. For the mass media, select those specific publications and stations you identified in the previous section. But also consider other ways of reaching that public. The chart in Chapter Eight of your text will provide some other options.

       For each public underline the two methods you believe would be MOST effective.

Publics Profile Chart

Based on the Claritas Prizm™ data

Public	What do you want this public to do as the result of your communications?	Where does this public live? List the zip codes and city.	What do you know about this public that will be useful for your campaign.	What media will reach this public?
1.				
2.				
3.				
4.				
5.				

Publics Profile Chart

Public	What do you want this public to do as the result of your communications?	Where does this public live? List the zip codes and city.	Based on the Claritas Prizm™ data	
			What do you know about this public that will be useful for your campaign.	What media will reach this public?
1.				
2.				
3.				
4.				
5.				

Public Relations Writing
Exercises and Assignments

This section includes exercises and writing assignments for all chapters in the text. The exercises will help you define your task, your publics and your strategy. The writing exercises provide practice in executing that strategy.

NOTE: In many cases the textbook web site at <www.sagepub.com/treadwell> includes assignments that will provide background and assistance in completing these exercises. It also includes active links to many of the sites referenced throughout this workbook. We suggest that you locate and review the website now and bookmark it on your computer. Because we will add to the site over time, we have not noted specific web resources in this workbook.

Exercises, Chapter One
Theoretical Influences on Public Relations Writing

■   Exercise 1-1: Current debates in public relations

The Internet makes it possible to follow the on-going debate regarding the definition and practice of public relations.

Use PRQuorum or other electronic forum to review current debates.

•   What topics are most hotly debated?

•   What issues might affect the public relations writing of the four clients in this text?

Exercises, Chapter Two
Sending the message: Writing for Style, Flow, and Credibility

■   Exercise 2.1: Transitions

Following are descriptions of advertising and public relations managers provided by the U.S. Bureau of Labor Statistics (www.bls.gov). The two descriptions appear separately and do not relate to each other. Combine them into a paragraph or two that compares and contrasts the two disciplines. Use transitional words and phrases to make the similarities and differences clear.

Description of Advertising Manager

Managers oversee advertising and promotion staffs, which usually are small, except in the largest firms. In a small firm, managers may serve as a liaison between the firm and the advertising or promotion agency to which many advertising or promotional functions are contracted out. In larger firms, advertising managers oversee in-house account, creative, and media services departments. The account executive manages the account services department, assesses the need for advertising, and, in advertising agencies, maintains the accounts of clients. The creative services department develops the subject matter and presentation of advertising. The creative director oversees the copy chief, art director, and associated staff. The media director oversees planning groups that select the communication media—for example, radio, television, newspapers, magazines, Internet, or outdoor signs—to disseminate the advertising.

Description of Public Relations Manager

   Public relations managers supervise public relations specialists. These managers direct publicity programs to a targeted public. They often specialize in a specific area, such as crisis management—or in a specific industry, such as healthcare. They use every available communication medium in their effort to maintain the support of the specific group upon whom their organization's success depends, such as consumers, stockholders, or the general public. For example, public relations managers may clarify or justify the firm's point of view on health or environmental issues to community or special interest groups.

   Public relations managers also evaluate advertising and promotion programs for compatibility with public relations efforts and serve as the eyes and ears of top management. They observe social, economic, and political trends that might ultimately affect the firm and make recommendations to enhance the firm's image based on those trends.

From U.S. Department of Labor Occupational Outlook Handbook http://stats.bls.gov/oco/ocos020.htm

■ Exercise 2.2: Parallel structure

   The four-paragraph section in Chapter Two that discusses parallel structure is written deliberately with many examples of parallel structure. List in the first column the start of each parallel construction (e.g., "from matching") and in the second column the element/s that parallel it (e.g., "to writing").

  _____   _____

  _____   _____

  _____   _____

  _____   _____

  _____   _____

  _____   _____

  _____   _____

  _____   _____

■ Writing Assignment 2-3: Application Letters

See also Plan of Attack Form

   NOW you are ready to write for your first client – yourself! Write a cover letter in response to one of the ads shown as Workbook Figure 2.4. All of these positions are entry-level, so previous paid writing or public relations work is not necessary. You should assume you are providing a résumé with this letter although the resumé is not the focus of this assignment. Please do not refer to any information you have about these clients except the ads.

   The letter should be no longer than one single-side page, single-spaced, and should represent your best effort to "sell" yourself to the organization. The following information and questions will guide you in producing an effective letter.

   Before you begin this section, be sure you have read the "Making Lemonade" panel in Chapter 2 of your text. And remember, this letter is to get you invited for an interview; it is unlikely to land you the job by itself.

COLLEGE PR SPECIALIST

Entry-level PR position available in busy college Communications Department. Position entails extensive writing in support of public affairs, college relations, alumni, admissions and development programs.

Successful applicant will be responsible for the weekly on-campus newsletter as well as for producing copy for: local media, alumni magazine, development solicitations, video and multi-media productions, college catalogs and recruitment brochures. It is expected that the appointee will also participate in the development and maintenance of the college website.

Applicants must be effective communicators. They will be required to demonstrate the ability to write news, feature and marketing copy. Familiarity with basic layout and print production will be a plus, as will knowledge of basic word processing and/or desktop publishing programs.

Please send cover letter detailing how your qualifications match our requirements to:

K. Kaman, Vice President of College Relations, Central College, 100 College Ave., Anytown, YS 11111

Public Relations Specialist

CommunicAID, a non-profit social services agency providing assistance for housing, employment, food, and education, requires a public relations specialist to support growing community affairs, education and development programs for the organization and its affiliate agencies.

Applicants must have a degree in communication or public relations and demonstrate the ability to write effective media releases as well as educational and marketing materials. A demonstrated interest in health, education or volunteer services will be a plus. A writing test will be required.

Please reply in writing, listing qualifications and reason for applying, to the Director of Human Resources.

COMMUNICAID

CARING FOR THE COMMUNITY
577 West Street
Anytown, YS 11111

POOR WRITERS NEED NOT APPLY!

We're a growing, regional internet service provider, and our Communications Department needs another good writer... *NOW!* We have a stack of projects waiting to be started -- like news stories on our growth, a good "how-to" manual for new users, and a web-letter to keep subscribers up to date. We're not short on PR ideas, just on people to translate them into action.

Experience is not necessary, but we *will* take a close look at your writing samples and give you a test that, frankly, most of our staff can't pass. That's why we need YOU!

Obviously, you should be familiar with computers, but we have plenty to people to train you on new programs.

So if you want a position where how good you are counts more than where (or if) you've worked before, send a letter to Alex Hale at the address below.

*1500 Century Drive
Suite 402
Anytown YS 11111*

Entry-level PR Specialist

Versatile writer wanted to help develop PR program for regional retail and mail-order company. Responsibilities will include writing and designing:

- media liaison;
- staff and client newsletters;
- brochures;
- annual report;
- conference support
- video scripts.

Position will also develop responses to client requests for proposals and participate as a member of the corporate marketing team.

Excellent communication skills a must. Applicants must be able to work independently. Familiarity with word-processing and design software (like MS Word and Quark Express) will be an asset.

Please send cover letter describing your qualifications to: S. Johnson, Recruitment Specialist, HealthWay Pharmacies, Inc., 1000 W. Main Street, Anytown, YS 11111

Applicants will be required to produce writing samples and take a company writing test.

HealthWay Pharmacies, Inc. is the largest chain of retail pharmacies in YS. It also offers prescription processing by mail, phone, EOE *fax or e-mail order.*

Workbook Figure 2.4: Recruitment ads for workbook clients.

1. Complete the Plan of Attack form for this exercise.

   The form will help ensure that you understand the project, audience, media and messages. It will also help you identify those aspects of your real experience that best support your ability to do the advertised job. It will help you match your skills and attributes with the organization's needs and to identify cogent evidence to support your claim that you can do the job better than anyone else.

2. Write the letter.

   Pay particular attention to style, flow and word choice. Read the letter aloud as you go to ensure the reader is led through the content and that it is strong and interesting.

   Present it as a formal, professional business letter with mastheads, addresses, type effects and signature, exactly as you would send it to a prospective employer.

3. Evaluate the letter

   After you have written a draft of the letter, compare it to the Plan of Attack form. Have you done what you set out to do? Is your evidence clear? Is it convincing? Is the letter itself a good advertisement for your skills?

Exercises, Chapter Three

Ethical Influences on Public Relations Writing

■ ## Exercise 3-1: Ethical decisions in public relations writing

As a means of encouraging communications, your college or university alumni office wants to offer alumni/ae the opportunity to link their personal web pages to the alumni office home page. The alumni office proposes to offer this service on its web site and through a form in the alumni magazine. They intend to link to the web sites of all alumni/ae who request it. The alumni office has asked for comment from the legal and public relations departments before implementing the program.

1. From a communications point of view you believe this is an excellent idea. From a public relations point of view, however, you anticipate some problems. At a minimum you believe some of the web sites might not reflect favorably on the institution.

   What ethical, and possibly legal, issues would influence your thinking for or against the project? Can you, for example, recommend that the alumni office screen all proposed web sites and link only to those that are approved? If so, what criteria should determine whether a site is approved or rejected? What about changes made in sites after they are approved? Try to think as broadly as possible. Knowing that all of the following alumni/ae have their own web pages should get you started.

   - An alumna who has contributed $5 million to the institution. What if she earned her fortune by producing pornographic videos?

   - An alumnus who has an ongoing lawsuit against the institution.

   - A former athlete who blames college trainers for mistreating an injury.

   - An alumnus who owns a chain of hardware stores.

- An alumnus who owns a chain of liquor stores.

- An alumna who owns a restaurant and winery.

- A former president of SADD, who is now president of the state chapter of Mothers Against Drunk Driving (MADD).

- An alumnus who is an active member of the NRA.

- An alumnus who is an active lobbyist for gun control.

- An alumna who is a convicted felon, currently serving a 25-year jail term.

- An alumnus who was accused and acquitted of child molestation.

- An alumnus who is public relations director of a competing institution.

2. Draft a memo to the alumni director setting out the ethical issues involved in proceeding with the project as planned. Write a one-paragraph policy governing the acceptance of web sites for linking that you believe will best protect the public relations of your institution. What ethical position is the basis for your policy?

3. Additionally the alumni office would like to offer the opportunity for alumni to purchase banner advertising on the pages sponsored by the alumni office (including on frames surrounding the home pages of other alumni). What ethical issues will arise if all ads are accepted? What if some are rejected? Write the guidelines for accepting or rejecting the content of advertising on alumni office pages.

■ Exercise 3-2: Mission statements

The web exercise for this chapter looks at the mission statements for several of the large, international public relations agencies.

Choose three of the agencies and, based on their mission statements (some are referred to as vision or values statements), answer the following questions:

1. What agencies did you select? Why?

2. What values do the agencies have in common? What values are different? What does this tell you about the public relations industry in general and about the agencies in particular?

3. What publics are the mission statements aimed at? What does this tell you about the agencies?

4. Which agency would you like to work for? Why? What values do you share with that agency?

■ **Writing Assignment 3.3: Client Mission Statements**

Although your client for this course has clearly-defined goals and standards, it is lacking a clear mission statement that will bring these goals and standards together in a way that its publics can understand and that the organization can use as guidance for its actions.

Your supervisor has asked each member of the Public Relations Department to write a draft mission statement for review and comment. Start by referring to the client's publics that you identified in the "Getting Started" section.

1. What ethical standards do these publics expect of your client?

2. What values will be important?

3. How does your client want to be thought of by each of these publics?

Combining these ideas with the organization's purpose in operating will give you the basis for a mission statement.

Write the mission statement for your client setting out the principles by which it will conduct operations and interact with its many publics.

Mission statements are typically concise. They flow smoothly with attention to rhythm and parallel structure. Go back to your draft mission statement and work on the choice of words, structure and flow so that it reflects a coherent, clear and memorable set of values and standards.

Exercises, Chapter Four

Cultural Influences on Public Relations Writing

■ Exercise 4-1: Characteristics of organizations

1. Following is a Semantic Differential scale using the attributes identified by Hofstede, Neuijen, Ohayv and Sanders. Based on the information and tone of your client's profile, position your client on these scales.

Open/Innovative	___	___	___	___	___	Closed to new ideas
Formal	___	___	___	___	___	Informal
Flexible	___	___	___	___	___	Rigid
People-focused	___	___	___	___	___	Product-focused
Impulsive	___	___	___	___	___	Cautious
Optimistic	___	___	___	___	___	Pessimistic
Involved	___	___	___	___	___	Isolated
Forward-looking	___	___	___	___	___	Grounded-in-the-past
Process Driven	___	___	___	___	___	Results Driven
Employee focused	___	___	___	___	___	Job focused
Collaborative	___	___	___	___	___	Hierarchical
Active	___	___	___	___	___	Passive

2. Which of the Deal and Kennedy categories described in Chapter 4 best describes your workbook client? Why?

3. How will the assessments you made in questions 1 and 2 above affect your writing?

■ **Writing Assignment** 4-2: Writing to reflect organizational culture

Corporate dress codes are obvious indicators of an organization's corporate culture. "Assignment: Organizational Culture" in your employer profile provides information regarding the adoption of an employee dress code by your employer. The information includes some background regarding how and why the dress code is being implemented or changed and some indications of what the dress code should be. It also includes a one-page sample of the current employee policy manual.

1.   Your task is to draft a new section to the employee policy manual explaining the new dress code. It will be inserted into the manual as a new section, so it must follow the style, both verbal and graphic, of the manual sample. Answering the following questions will help you complete this project.

  •   What is/are the audience/s for this assignment? If there are multiple audiences, is the message the same to all of them? Why or why not? What will the audience think of the message?

  •   Do you need any additional information to complete this assignment? If so, who/what is the most appropriate source of the information?

          Does this assignment fit into your employer's goals? Into your public relations writing plan? Remember that some communications respond to outside forces. They may or may not be related to an organizational goal or objective.

  •   How does corporate culture play a role in this assignment? How does it affect what you write? How do you know what tone or vocabulary to use?

  •   How will you know if your writing is effective?

2.   This draft will be reviewed by your supervisor and then the President/CEO. Prepare a memo that will serve as a cover to the dress code draft. Remember especially the style and presentation issues that you determined were appropriate for the letter of application to this employer in Chapter Two.

■   Exercise 4-3: Intercultural opportunities

1.   Conduct a web search to identify at least six sites in different industries that offer multi-language options. Try to find at least one that is related to your client's industry.

Organization   Web site

_____   _____

_____   _____

_____   _____

_____   _____

_____   _____

2.   What cultural groups might your client be interested in? Pay special attention to the demographic information you identified in the "Getting Started" exercise.

3.   The most recent census indicates that the ethnic breakdown of the greater Anytown region has changed from 20 percent Hispanic to 50 percent Hispanic, with reductions in all other ethnic groups. Look carefully at the location of your client's operations and the programs your client has in place or wants to participate in. What communication strategies (if any) would you recommend that your client adopt in light of this change?

Exercises, Chapter Five

Research Influences on Public Relations Writing

■ Exercise 5-1: Web research: key words

Explore the differences in search engines by using a common search term such as "public relations writing" on three different search engines.

Now try using the terms "printer," "printing," and "commercial printing" on a single search engine. You should notice a great difference in the search results. What do these searches tell you about the importance of key words in searches and in creating web sites of your own?

■ Exercise 5.2: Researching the environment, client, publics and media

The basic exercises for identifying client, environment, media and publics information are included in the "Getting Started" section of this workbook. Following are supplementary exercises that will tell you more about each of these topics.

1.   Researching the environment, additional information

Broadly speaking, environmental research is identifying the issues, trends, factors and institutions that affect or potentially affect your client's ability to operate. For public relations writing in particular, these factors include the size and nature of your market, organizations that can help or compete with you, legal support or constraints and social issues relevant to your client.

In the "Getting Started" section you identified organizations that one might consider competitors to your client. List three types of information you want to know about these competitors that will affect your public relations writing

2.   Researching your client

Much of the information you will need about your client has been provided in the client profile at the beginning of this workbook. You should read this profile carefully so that you are familiar with the people, places and details you will use again and again in your writing.

What information not available in the client profile do you think you will need in order to write effective copy for your client? Where do you expect to get this information?

Information   Source

_____   _____

_____   _____

_____   _____

3.   Researching your client's publics

Understanding publics is, arguably, one of the most important aims of the research you will conduct for any client. Sources for information about these publics will be both formal and informal. It will be based on what you know about your client and what you know about the sector and indeed, the competition. In the "Getting Started" section of this workbook, you identified many demographic characteristics of the region in which your client operates and also some characteristics about individual publics. Following are some additional questions you may want to answer.

- What other information will you need to know about these publics in order to write effective copy for your client? Where will you get this information?

Information   Source

_____   _____
_____   _____
_____   _____
_____   _____
_____   _____

- Public image: What do these publics think of your client?

  In the "Getting Started" section you identified many publics with whom your client might have or want a relationship. List the publics below. Although you have not done any formal research at this point, you can make an educated guess as to what these publics might think. What do you think is the attitude of each of these publics toward your client?

Public   Attitude

_____	Positive	Neutral	Negative	Unaware
_____	Positive	Neutral	Negative	Unaware
_____	Positive	Neutral	Negative	Unaware
_____	Positive	Neutral	Negative	Unaware
_____	Positive	Neutral	Negative	Unaware
_____	Positive	Neutral	Negative	Unaware
_____	Positive	Neutral	Negative	Unaware
_____	Positive	Neutral	Negative	Unaware
_____	Positive	Neutral	Negative	Unaware
_____	Positive	Neutral	Negative	Unaware
_____	Positive	Neutral	Negative	Unaware

- What do these attitudes tell you about the writing you will do for your client? For example, will writing targeted to your priority publics be primarily informative or persuasive, grade school level or college level, detailed or simple?

4.   Researching messages

   •   Research national and local media to find at least three articles about your client's sector. What messages are being published about this sector?

Message	Source	Type of article	
		News	Opinion
_____	_____	_____	_____
_____	_____	_____	_____
_____	_____	_____	_____

   •   How would you characterize these messages: positive, negative, educational, persuasive?

Message	Type of article		Attitude	
	Educational	Persuasive	Positive	Negative
_____	_____	_____	_____	_____
_____	_____	_____	_____	_____
_____	_____	_____	_____	_____

   •   Which of these messages (if any) do you think resulted from the organization's or sector's public relations effort? What makes you think so?

5.   Researching effects

Effects research typically comes after the project is complete. But you should define in advance what results/effects you will be seeking.

   For each public you identified earlier, what do you think will be the major purpose(s) of your communications: knowledge, attitude or behavior change? At the end of a project, you will want to know whether your communication achieved these purposes. Your client's mission and goals, and the attitudes you circled under "Publics Research" above should help you define these purposes.

Identifying the purpose of communicating with each public

Public	Communication Purpose		
_____	Knowledge	Attitude	Behavior
_____	Knowledge	Attitude	Behavior
_____	Knowledge	Attitude	Behavior
_____	Knowledge	Attitude	Behavior
_____	Knowledge	Attitude	Behavior
_____	Knowledge	Attitude	Behavior
_____	Knowledge	Attitude	Behavior
_____	Knowledge	Attitude	Behavior
_____	Knowledge	Attitude	Behavior

Exercises, Chapter Six

Legal Influences on Public Relations Writing

■   <u>Exercise 6-1: Protecting privacy in public relations communications</u>

Federal and state governments, departments and agencies make information on laws and regulations available on their web sites. Research the Internet and/or your institution's library to identify federal and state laws governing the release of information held by your text client. A good place to start is the U.S.s government site: <fedlaw.gsa.gov> and the web sites of the Department(s) and the industry and trade associations that most closely relate to the client.

If you cannot identify an appropriate law, attempt to find a relevant bill before Congress or guidelines on the subject in other web sites. The Fedlaw web site has user-friendly search engines and from it you can access both federal and state laws and regulations.

Following are some common situations in which public relations practitioners might be asked to provide information to the media or for use in promotions or by other organizations. In each case determine if it is legal to release the information (i.e., "can you" release it?) and if it is ethical and/or good public relations strategy to release it (i.e., "would you" release it?)   Be prepared to answer why or why not in each case.

	Can you release?	Would you release?
• Your college's *overall* student loan default rate	_____	_____
• A list of alumni from your college who have defaulted on their loans	_____	_____
• The academic records of members of your college's baseball team	_____	_____
• John Smith's on-campus criminal record	_____	_____
• Last year's crime statistics for your college	_____	_____
• The names of residents of a homeless shelter	_____	_____
• Statistics about the residents of a homeless shelter	_____	_____
• A list of your subscribers to a company that sells mailing lists	_____	_____
• A list of your company's clients for your promotional brochure	_____	_____
• A candid photo of a client for use in your promotional brochure	_____	_____
• The names of celebrities for whom you have filled prescriptions	_____	_____
• The prescriptions you filled for a given, named person	_____	_____
• Printing in the annual report an identifiable photo of an individual	_____	_____
• That a named person has been terminated	_____	_____
• That a named person was terminated because she was HIV positive	_____	_____

■ <u>Exercise 6-2: Monitoring legislation that affects your writing</u>

In order to protect your client's compliance with laws and regulations, it is wise to monitor legislation that may affect your client's industry. To get you started, we suggest searching the web sites listed in the chapter and using standard search engines using words and phrases such as: privacy, confidentiality, credit reporting, medical records, patient records, debt collections, educational records, spamming, Internet privacy, to name but a few. HINT: The Fedlaw web site will be especially useful for this assignment.

1. Identify at least three current laws and regulations that have provisions regarding privacy and/or the confidentiality of information or ownership or trademarks, etc., that may be relevant to your text client. Record the numbers and web site or database information below.

Law/topic	Number/section	Location (web/library)
_____	_____	_____
_____	_____	_____
_____	_____	_____
_____	_____	_____

2. Identify at least three bills which have been presented to the current or most recent session of Congress that have provisions related to privacy or the confidentiality of information or ownership of trademarks, etc., that will affect your Workbook client. Record the numbers and web site or database information on the following chart.

Law/topic	Number/section	Location (web/library)
_____	_____	_____
_____	_____	_____
_____	_____	_____
_____	_____	_____

Exercises, Chapter Seven

<u>Design Influences on Public Relations Writing</u>

■ <u>Exercise 7-1: Exploring layouts</u>

A good way to understand symmetric and asymmetric layouts and to explore how your client's logo and corporate style will impact your layout choices is to design a business card. It should include the organization's logo (if there is one) and name as well as the name and title of the cardholder and his or her contact information: mailing address, e-mail address and telephone and fax numbers. Many business cards also include a web site address.

1. Following are four blank horizontal cards for you to design one symmetric and three asymmetric designs. They should be designed in black and white, including shades of gray. Note that

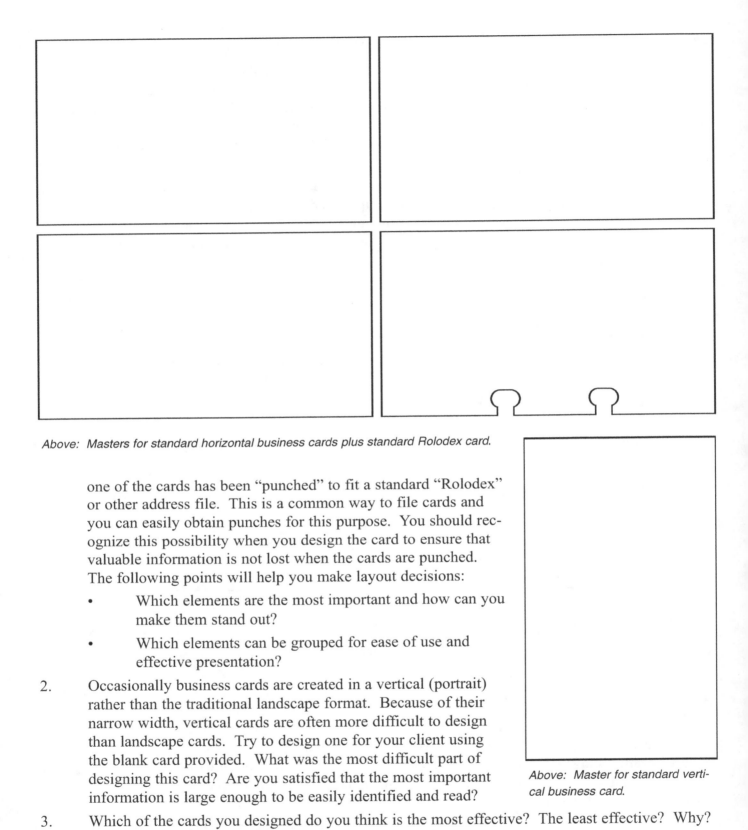

Above: Masters for standard horizontal business cards plus standard Rolodex card.

one of the cards has been "punched" to fit a standard "Rolodex" or other address file. This is a common way to file cards and you can easily obtain punches for this purpose. You should recognize this possibility when you design the card to ensure that valuable information is not lost when the cards are punched. The following points will help you make layout decisions:

- Which elements are the most important and how can you make them stand out?

- Which elements can be grouped for ease of use and effective presentation?

2. Occasionally business cards are created in a vertical (portrait) rather than the traditional landscape format. Because of their narrow width, vertical cards are often more difficult to design than landscape cards. Try to design one for your client using the blank card provided. What was the most difficult part of designing this card? Are you satisfied that the most important information is large enough to be easily identified and read?

Above: Master for standard vertical business card.

3. Which of the cards you designed do you think is the most effective? The least effective? Why?

Exercise 7-2: Effective charts and graphs

In your client's profile, we have provided a page of financial information, including a financial statement and some growth statistics. You may assume this information is current and that it will be the basis for the annual report you may produce later in this course. Create at least two charts or graphs for this annual report. One should illustrate this year's financial position compared to last year's. One should illustrate a growth statistic that will be relevant to the following audience:

*   CommunicAID....................the Anytown Community
*   Central College ....Alumni
*   HealthWay Pharmacies ......Clients, insurance providers, the Anytown business community.
*   ValleyLINK:........................Client subscribers and companies whose web sites ValleyLINK hosts

Exercise 7-3: Color selection for image and purpose

Most large organizations include the PMS color specifications for their corporate logos, signage, names, etc. in their organizational style manual and then require all persons preparing documents to be printed by commercial printers to use the approved PMS colors. At best these colors were likely the subject of many debates at executive level before the final choice was made and most organizations that have spent time and money developing a corporate image guard it carefully.

To this point your client has not designated color(s) as part of its "corporate" style. This has resulted in uncoordinated documents produced in the favorite colors of the purchasing agents, marketing specialists and public relations staff who order stationery, brochures and marketing materials.

1. Your CEO/president now wants recommendations for a two-color combination that will be appropriate for all of the organization's documents: business cards/stationery, folders, brochures, newsletters, annual reports, web site, etc. These colors may be used together as a two-color combination or as a three-color combination including black. You should use these colors for the rest of the design projects in this text. What colors would you recommend? Why?

2. Re-design two of the business card layouts that you designed in Exercise 7-1, using the new organizational colors that you selected above.

Company name, your name, number, email, title (PR specialist), company website. logo, slogan,

Above: Masters for standard horizontal business cards for color design.

Exercise 7-4: Presentation folders

1.   Design a presentation folder for your client to use as a press kit for special functions. Human Resources has also indicated a desire to use it for employee orientation packets.

   - Consider the design elements that you used for the business cards you designed. Try to achieve a unified look that will become your client's image or "signature."

   - You must use the organizational colors you defined in Exercise 7-3.

   - How does knowing your client's culture and mission affect the design?

   - How does knowing your priority/major audiences affect the design?

Exercises, Chapter Eight

From Principles to Planning to Practice: Business Writing, Fact Sheets, Bios

Writing Assignment 8-1: Report writing

Following are three situations that typically will require a public relations writer to research and produce a report. Select one of the topics and write a three to five page report. You have already done the necessary research in Chapters Three to Six.

The Expanded Report Format should provide the scope you need to present the information effectively and to create headings appropriate to the topic and your findings. You may choose whether to present it in the order shown or to begin with "Conclusions" for example. The only required section is an Executive Summary. Be selective about the information you include in the report. For this assignment it is more important that the topics you choose are covered comprehensively than that you cover every possible topic. Three to five pages should be sufficient for you to demonstrate your understanding of report writing.

Be prepared to discuss why you structured the report the way you did, i.e., why you chose particular headings and sub-headings to organize the body of the report.

1.   Several weeks ago the Vice President/Director of Administration for your text client brought to the executive committee (President/CEO, all vice presidents and all directors) an article about the growing concern of Congress over the ownership of information, both the public's right to privacy in personal records and the right of organizations to logos, documents etc. used as part of the organizational identity. The executive committee asked you to research these issues as they affect your text client and to write a report on your findings.

   At a minimum, the report should cover existing laws, proposed changes (and their status), some comment or background on why the issue is important to Congress and to your client and how any changes will affect your client. You did the research for this project in Chapter Six.

2.   As your client approaches a new financial year, management is looking at all departments to determine how next year's budget allocations should be made. Your task is to provide a report on the public relations program, specifically addressing the question of how the program ensures that all of the client's publics receive information that meets their needs.

The report may identify the publics, their needs and their opinion of the organization, show if and why these publics are important and discuss how the organization can communicate with them. It should include recommendations for reaching at least the three most important publics. No costings or budget estimates are necessary. The research for this project was done in the "Getting Started" project.

3.   Your client has asked for a synthesis of the organization to be used as a resource for the new executives the organization expects to recruit in a few months. The report may include topics such as the organization's mission.

■ Writing Assignment 8-2: Fact sheets

See also Plan of Attack Form

Your client is expecting a visit to its headquarters by a group of aides to the elected members of the YourState legislature. This group is on a two-week tour to familiarize themselves with what goes on in your region of the state and to help them identify sources of information about future legislative actions. In order to create a level playing field for all organizations regardless of their size, financial status or employment numbers, the aides have stipulated that the only hard-copy information that they will accept during the tour are fact sheets (one page both sides).

Create a fact sheet about your client for this occasion. You should incorporate into it at least one statistic or technical fact that you "translate" into an example familiar to the public. Think, for example, about the number of people eligible for or participating in a program, or dollars raised or put back into the local economy (at the rate of $30,000 for every employee). The point is that these numbers don't mean anything. Find an analogy that will make them meaningful.

1.   First complete the Plan of Attack form for this exercise. It will help you define your audience and style and identify and organize information for the fact sheet.

2.   Write the fact sheet. Present it with simple type effects or graphics as you would want it to appear in finished form.

3.   Evaluate the fact sheet

■ Writing Assignment 8-3: Boilerplates

Part of effective planning for public relations writing is to recognize when something you have written previously can be used as is or quickly adapted to fill another purpose. For example, you will have many opportunities to use a boilerplate paragraph about an organization – as part of a fact sheet, at the end of news releases, as part of a brochure, and in the program of conferences you may attend, for example.

Write a boilerplate paragraph now so that you will have it ready for these future exercises. The information you learned when writing the fact sheet in the previous assignment should be everything you need to know for this boilerplate paragraph. In fact, if you include in this paragraph a fact that you did not include in the fact sheet, you should ask yourself "why?"and review the fact sheet to see if it should be included.

■ **Writing Assignment 8-4: Bios**

You will need a bio of your employer's senior executive (president or CEO) to include in grant or new business proposals, as a hand-out to the press before he or she speaks at the special event your client may sponsor and possibly for the organization's web site.

Write this bio now so you have it available when you need it. It should be no longer than one page and should be written as a narrative style.

The following information is the basis of the bio. It may be adapted to suit the president or CEO of any of the workbook clients You may also use information from your client's profile and invent details as appropriate for your client's industry.

* Education: ....BS: YourCollege, Anytown, YourState (graduated cum laude).

    ....Graduate degree/s (as appropriate): University of YourState.

* Experience: ....Total job history: 25 years including at least two employers starting at a junior position and rising through two management positions to the current leadership. Also spent three summers working at a local camp during college.

* Leadership: ....Holds at least one office in a relevant local or industry association.

* Personal: ....Has been named "Executive of the Year" by a relevant association for business and philanthropic activities.

Exercises, Chapter Nine
Out of Your Control ... or is it? News writing for the Press

■ Exercise 9-1: Public relations news in the press

1. To see what news values determine local story placements, read and analyze at least one issue of a local daily newspaper. Working with the local, feature (e.g., lifestyle, leisure, etc.) and business sections, identify those stories that you believe originated with a public relations source.

    Stories with PR origin   Source

    _____   _____

    _____   _____

    _____   _____

    _____   _____

    _____   _____

    _____   _____

    _____   _____

    _____   _____

    _____   _____

- How can you recognize a story that originated with a public relations source?
- Compute the number of public relations-sourced stories as a percentage of the total number of stories on those pages.
- What percentage of the stories you analyzed appear to have public relations origins?

2. Write below six "good news" topics that your client might consider publicizing.

_____   _____
_____   _____
_____   _____

- Which of these topics is likely to be of interest to the local media in the Anytown region?
- Which, if any, would be of interest to national media, to specialized media? Why?
- What would make each story newsworthy e.g., what is the determinant?

3. Conduct a web or media directory search to identify at least one specialty publication that might be interested in your client's industry and/or achievements.

■ Exercise 9.2: Client attitudes toward the media

Organizations vary greatly in their attitudes toward media coverage. Some, such as debt collectors are understandably shy, having been "burned" by a misquote or unfavorable article. Others eagerly seek media attention, and have staffs to write releases, pitch story ideas and answer media questions.

1. How might the following affect an organization's interest in media coverage?
- Location and distribution of its publics, e.g., local or distant, in one region or scattered.
- Public image of competitors, e.g., high profile/low profile.
- Concern for protecting plans and results from competitors.
- Need for public funding.

Which of these would influence your client's attitude toward the media? What other factors would influence it?

2. In your experience, what is the attitude of the general public toward the industries of the clients in this text? Plot out the likely attitudes for all of them on the following chart.

	Very positive	Positive	Neutral	Negative	Very negative
Non-profit organizations	____	____	____	____	____
Retail pharmacies	____	____	____	____	____
Colleges and universities	____	____	____	____	____
Internet service providers	____	____	____	____	____

- What role do you think the media has played (if any) in shaping these opinions?
- How do you think these opinions will affect each client's attitudes toward cooperation with the media?

- Based on your considerations above, which client(s) are most likely to want regular or frequent media coverage? Which client(s) might be wary of media attention? Why?
- Which of the clients is/are most likely to be the subject of regular media attention? Why? What topics might be of interest?

■ Exercise 9.3: Reviewing releases for purpose and style

Checking for purpose and professionalism - Figures 9.2 and 9.6 in the text are media releases issued by Girls Incorporated and Alteon Training L.L.C. Review them carefully to assess their physical layout, news values and balance. Score them on the following scale:

	Girls Inc.	Alteon
Layout (Score one point on each category - maximum total of 10)		
• Page/story ends with "More," "ends," "30" or "XXX"	_____	_____
• Contact Information:		
- Name	_____	_____
- Work Phone #	_____	_____
- Home Phone #	_____	_____
- Fax #	_____	_____
- E-mail Address &/or web site address	_____	_____
- Release date	_____	_____
- Dateline	_____	_____
- Headline or space for editor to write headline	_____	_____
• Clean, ,error-free, typed copy	_____	_____
News Values (Rank out of ten points) (10 = strong, 1= weak)	_____	_____
News structure (inverted pyramid) rank out of ten points	_____	_____
Public relations message		
• (Score 10 if it meets the needs of both media and organization, and 0 if it meets the needs of only one of them.)	_____	_____
TOTAL POINTS OUT OF 40	_____	_____

■ **Writing Assignment 9-4: Writing press releases**

Also see Plan of Attack Form

The background information for the "News Writing" assignment in your client's profile presents a situation for which your client wants media coverage. It is the announcement of an event that is "good news" such as a new project, contract or award. Your client wants to capitalize on it immediately. We have provided the scenario and additional background information including the effect this event will have on your organization. You may assume that your employer's executives and/or other appropriate parties have agreed to be quoted in the release and you may draft one or more brief quotes as appropriate.

1. First complete the Plan of Attack form for this exercise. It will help you understand what is news about your story and how to ensure the media recognizes the news. It will also help you ensure that you send a public relations message in the story as well.

2. Write the press release.

   Present it exactly as if you were sending it to the media on behalf of your client, including all of the elements of a press release shown in your text.

3. Evaluate the press release.

■ ## **Writing Assignment 9-5: Pitch letters**

Also see Plan of Attack Form

Following are revised scenarios for the announcement of your employer's "Good News".

- Central College — The President of Central College, the President of the Anytown School District, and 20 high school sophomores who have voluntarily signed up for the program are available for a news conference to announce the start of the "Early Support" program. The computer facilities at the college, at the college annex and at Anytown High School are available for the conference.

- CommunicAID — The CommunicAID president and the Anytown Mayor have agreed to announce the new Mercer Street center at a joint news conference at the Mercer School. Plans for the center will be available at that time. The school cafeteria and the Pre-K annex are both in good condition. Either can be used for this press conference.

- HealthWay Pharmacies — The director of the YSEA health insurance program and the Othertown Mayor are both available for a press conference to announce the awarding of the YSEA contract and the availability of this new service to YSEA members. Any of the HealthWay Pharmacies premises can be used for the event.

- ValleyLINK — The President of ValleyLINK and the Midstate Health Director of Mental Health Services have agreed to cut the ribbon on the first "SeniorLink" computer site, at the Midstate Health Senior Center in Anytown. The local computer teacher has agreed to provide five computer-literate fifth graders who are working on a project on the history of their home town to act as the other end of the link with the seniors.

1. First complete the plan of attack form for this project. In it you will select several media outlets that will be interested in the story and identify different "pitches" that would be unique to each.

2. Write a pitch letter.

   Choose one or two media, or special reporters (e.g., business, science, etc.) you believe will be interested in the story and that will reach key publics with the story. The pitch letter should make clear the unique "angle" that will interest each of them to attend the event and cover the story themselves. You may assign a date, time and place for the event.

3. Evaluate the pitch letter.

Exercises, Chapter Ten

Under Your Control: Features and Newsletters

Most features written by public relations writers are used for internal documents rather than written for the external media. This is good news for the writer because it means that the story will be used as you have written it. Plus, whenever you can tailor copy to a particular known audience (as is the case with newsletter copy) you will enjoy creative license that you do not have with routine media copy.

Two key uses for public relations features are annual reports and newsletters. In annual reports, the feature usually develops the theme of the report. In newsletters, the feature may be related to personnel, historical, business or social issues. This all adds to the fun of feature writing. If you are responsible for a regular newsletter, you may find yourself in the enviable position of identifying subjects for and writing many features.

■ ## Exercise 10-1: Identifying features

1. Based on the information provided in the background material for your client and on the mission statement you wrote, answer the following questions:

    • How do you expect your client will feel about feature articles versus about news articles? For the mass media? For internal publications?

    • How might the time of year affect your client's interest in a feature story?

    • Do you expect local media to use a feature story you write? Why? Why not?

2. For your client, identify topics that might lead to a feature story. The information provided in your client profile and background information will help you determine the topics. To help you begin we have listed the types of features discussed in this section. Identify all the media for which each feature would be appropriate.

Story type	Your client topic	Internal newsltr	External newsltr	Annual report	Other media
Employee feature	_____	____	____	____	____
Case study	_____	____	____	____	____
Case history	_____	____	____	____	____
Research finding	_____	____	____	____	____
Backgrounder	_____	____	____	____	____
Educational	_____	____	____	____	____
Supplement to news story	_____	____	____	____	____
By-liner (for whom?)	_____	____	____	____	____
Other	_____	____	____	____	____

3. How does each of these topics fit into the organization's communication plan?

■ Writing Assignment 10-2: The feature story

Also see Plan of Attack Form

In Exercise 9-4, you wrote a press release announcing a new project or contract your client was about to undertake. For the purpose of this assignment, assume that the project has been underway for a year and that your client wants to publish a human-interest feature story derived from that project in a newsletter or an annual report which will be sent to the following audience. (Your instructor will tell you which.)

If you are writing for a newsletter, assume that it will be a special issue focusing on your organization's involvement in the community. If you are writing for an annual report, the theme of the annual report will be: "Strengthening the Community." In both cases the feature should illustrate or support the theme although it does not have to be the theme of the story itself.

Employer	External newsletter and annual report target audiences
• Central College	Annual fund donors: alumni, friends, parents, faculty.
• CommunicAID	The Anytown community
• HealthWay	Company clients, insurance providers, the Anytown business community
• ValleyLINK	Subscribers and users of the ValleyLINK service: i.e., ValleyLINK clients

Refer to the background for the "Feature Writing" assignment in your employer profile. In this assignment, we have provided information you could use for such a feature, including facts and statistics about the project and comments from people involved. You may also use some of the information provided in the "News Writing" assignment and that you used in your news release. The information should open up a wide range of possibilities for feature stories about each client.

1. First complete the Plan of Attack form for this exercise. It will help you identify a theme and technique you can use to develop the feature for this target audience.

2. Write three lead paragraphs for the story using three different techniques. Which do you like best? Why? Which is most appropriate for your target public? Why?

3. Write the story. Aim for at least two double-spaced pages to demonstrate your feature style.

4. Evaluate the feature story.

■ Exercise 10-3: Understanding newsletter audiences

It is likely that the four workbook clients will regard employee newsletters differently.

1. Which client/s, if any, do you think would be likely to publish more than one employee newsletter? (HINT: think about vertical distribution)? Why?

2. Which clients might publish more than one external newsletter? To whom?

3. Consider only your own client to answer the following questions:

   • Identify four divisions or levels of employees. What is the probable education level of each of these groups? What level of occupational specialization do you see (low, average or high)?

   NOTE: Students working for CommunicAID should include the organization's non-profit affiliates as part of their staff. Complete the following chart to determine whether these four groups are sufficiently different to warrant their own publications.

Employee group	Education level	Level of specialization
_____	_____	_____
_____	_____	_____
_____	_____	_____
_____	_____	_____

- Are these employees different enough and is your total audience large enough to produce separate newsletters for each group or at least for more than one group? If so, identify the audience for each publication.

■ Exercise 10-4: Newsletter planning

The background to the assignment "Newsletters" in your client profile includes ideas and some raw material for an employee newsletter and an external newsletter. These will be the first issues after the new year.

1. Identify which articles you expect to use in each publication and complete the chart below. Also determine the approach (type of writing) – news, feature, instructional or persuasive – that you will use for each article.

   HINT: Consider whether you can combine some items. For example, think about using standard formats and headings for information that is repeated each month like new staff, promotions, and births, deaths, marriages, illnesses, etc. Special headings or columns can save you a lot of space and explanations. They also provide a good chance to use graphics or typographic elements to make the publication more visually interesting.

Employee newsletter		External newsletter	
Article/topic	Approach	Article/topic	Approach
_____	_____	_____	_____
_____	_____	_____	_____
_____	_____	_____	_____
_____	_____	_____	_____
_____	_____	_____	_____
_____	_____	_____	_____
_____	_____	_____	_____
_____	_____	_____	_____
_____	_____	_____	_____

- Put an asterisk next to three articles you want to print on the front page.
- Put a check mark next to the three least important articles for each newsletter. These will be the first articles cut if you do not have space.

2. The following exercises 10-5 through 10-7 provide practice in several styles of writing common to newsletters: news, highlights or bullet points, and special columns. It is also likely that you could adapt the feature article you wrote in Exercise 10-2 for a newsletter.

■ **Writing Assignment 10-5: News writing for newsletters**

Also see Plan of Attack Form

In a previous assignment, you wrote a news release on a good news topic that your client wanted to release to the general public. That does not mean that you would not use the same story in internal or external newsletters. To the contrary, it is common that such stories would be front-page news on newsletters even if the press had already printed them. The point is that the stories will be different from the media release. Ways in which they may differ include:

* Content – there will be details of interest to employees especially and possibly to friends of the organization that will not be of interest to the general public.

* Spokesperson – the person who will resonate most with employees, for example, may be unknown to the general public.

* Style – even newsletters aimed at an external audience tend not to be as formal as news releases. Certainly they are not bound by the conventions of media style and formatting. You are free to write in a style that is appropriate to the audience, even to cross the boundaries between news and feature style to create interesting, attention-getting articles.

* Purpose – the purpose of a newsletter is always to make the recipients feel closer to the organization, so the purpose of individual articles is to help achieve this, i.e., to make readers feel special, as if they know something that the general public does not.

Look again at the information provided as background to the media release. There should be some information you did not find suitable for a media release. Consider again if it is suitable for an employee newsletter. It is also likely that you will want to use different quotes (and possible a different spokesperson) as you "speak" to an audience of "family-members".

1. Begin by completing the Plan of Attack form for this assignment.

    It will help you determine appropriate content, tone and contents for a newsletter article.

2. Write the newsletter article for an employee audience.

3. Nominate any photos you would expect to run with the article.

4. Evaluate the article against your aims in the Plan of Attack form and the requirements above.

■ **Writing Assignment 10-6: Bullet Points in Newsletters**

Bullet points are effective ways to organize newsletter copy, much of which is often very brief. Review the topics you have determined would make an effective newsletter and also the background information provided for newsletters in your client's profile. Identify those items that would be effectively presented as in "highlights" or bullet-point format. There should be a common theme under which they can be grouped.

1. Write the heading you want to use for this bullet-point section.

2. Identify the points that support the headline.

3. Review the list and rewrite to ensure that the bullet points match each other in style and that they all continue naturally from the heading.

■ Writing Assignment 10-7: The CEO message

Newsletters are one of the few ways organizations have for communicating regularly with publics, and for their chief executives to become known to many publics. Accordingly, it is common for newsletters, both internal and external, to include regular columns "written by" the organization's president, CEO or other officer. These messages are usually topical and upbeat, although when necessary they may be used to provide personal reassurance about an issue or topic that is negative.

1. Who will "sign" the message? It should not be you, even in your role as editor. Unless the newsletter is very large, it is rare for the editor to "speak" in it.

2. What is this person's personality? What traits do you want to reflect in the message? How can you do this?

3. What do you believe key audiences for this newsletter want to know from an organizational executive?

4. Write a one-column (about 300 words) message from the person you identified above. The profile for your organization provides some guidance on the topic, and the topic and the person's personality will guide the tone.

5. What photo and/or graphics would you suggest should accompany the column?

■ Exercise 10-8: Newsletter design to support your message

Newsletters should have a consistent appearance across multiple editions so that they are instantly recognizable and so that readers know where to look for features they especially like, much as you know where to find the sports, comics or television listings in the daily newspaper.

In addition, you need a size and format that you are confident of filling every issue and that will facilitate distribution. For this exercise you will plan and design the employee newsletter for which you have already written the copy. Answer the following questions as a preliminary to this design exercise.

*   How many pages do you expect you would be able to fill every issue?

*   How often do you want to publish the newsletter?

*   How will the newsletter be distributed? Don't forget that self-mailers will need space for mailing addresses and will probably be folded.

*   What paper size will you choose: e.g., 17" x 11" folded to 8.5" x 11", four pages 8.5" x 11" folded, unfolded, multiple-page stapled?

*   What color(s) if any, will you recommend? What font(s)?

*   What method of reproduction will you use?

Design the first two pages of the employee newsletter to show the basic design you will retain for each issue. These pages must have at least: the masthead, CEO/president's column, a lead story, work and social information, contact information. Indicate positions for photos and graphics.

Exercises, Chapter Eleven

Let's Hear It! Writing for Broadcast, Scripts and Speeches

■   Exercise 11-1: Public relations news on broadcast media

This exercise will help you think about the potential of television news as a medium for telling your client's story. It should give you a sense of how appealing your client is as news content and how much time you might be able to obtain on a typical news program, if your story is judged to be newsworthy by the editor.

1.   Watch two half-hour news broadcasts on local TV stations and complete the following chart for each broadcast, listing all stories and the time they begin and end. Try to select a broadcast time slot that you know has local interest or "soft"news. Include the total times for each commercial break and for sports and weather. Then answer the questions following the chart.

Story subject	Start time	End time	Duration

•   How much program time is available overall (program time = program length minus commercial time)?

•   How much *news* time is available overall (news time = program time minus time for weather and sports segments?)   This news time is what you will be trying to "claim" for your client.

- How many stories were aired during this news time? On average, how long did each news story last?

3. What does this tell you about where most public relations writers are likely to put their efforts? The time available is even less on radio.

4. What broadcast media do you think would be interested in stories about your client? Why?

■ Writing Assignment 11-2: Writing for broadcast

Also see Plan of Attack Form

To understand the difference between printed (press) copy and broadcast copy, it is necessary to be able to hear what you write. This exercise asks to you look again at "Good News" press release you wrote in Exercise 9-4, and to turn it into a release that broadcast editors would be able to use. Refer to the press release you wrote in Exercise 9-4, announcing your client's good news. Read it aloud. Seriously, read it out loud; tape it if possible.

- How many minutes does it take to read? How many minutes should it take?

- Is it easy to read? Does it sound like you are speaking naturally?

- Are the words easy to pronounce? What about the proper names?

- Do you know where to pause and take a breath? Are the sentences too long to be read easily in one breath? Are they so short that they are choppy?

1. Now complete the Plan of Attack Form for this project

It will help you identify words, phrases and sentences of your release that need rewriting or special treatment for use by radio or TV news readers.

2. Rewrite the news release for a 1-minute broadcast spot.

Use the styles discussed in this chapter and broadcast stylebooks and the formatting information provided in this chapter to make the release suitable for reading by a news reader. Read and time it to ensure it is a 1-minute spot.

3. Now write it for a 30-second radio spot.

4. Evaluate the releases.

■ Writing Assignment 11-3: Scriptwriting

Also see Plan of Attack Form

Your client has determined that a brief video would be useful for enough projects (as described below) to warrant the expense of producing it. You are now in charge of the project. (You should be enthused; this should be fun, and indicates that your client has confidence in your abilities.)

The video will be five to seven minutes long and can range from graphics only to videotaped action. You may use your client's facilities and staff as necessary in the video. The purpose of the video will be informational, educational and/or persuasive.

Non-profit clients (e.g., CommunicAID and Central College) will use the video to support requests for funding, to accompany written grant requests, to supplement speeches given by organizational executives, and to provide interest at conferences at which the organization exhibits.

Commercial clients (HealthWay and ValleyLINK) will use the video to support written new business proposals, to support speeches given by company executives and to provide interest at trade fairs where the company is exhibiting.

1. First, complete the Plan of Attack form for this project.

    It will help you narrow a theme, develop a logical flow, and decide on speakers, locations and action.

2. Write the script for the video.

    Read it aloud to ensure it is 5-7 minutes long and that it sounds natural.

3. Create a storyboard for the video including the script and drawings or descriptions of the visuals. Indicate whether the visuals are still photos, drawings, or video footage of people talking or in action. We have provided blank storyboard templates for this project.

4. Evaluate the project.

■ Writing Assignment 11-4: Speechwriting

Also see Plan of Attack Form

During the visit of the YourState legislative aides you prepared a fact sheet in Exercise 8-2. In addition, your organization's president or CEO has the opportunity to give a 10-minute speech on the topic "Who are you and what can your legislators do for you?" The "you" in question is, of course, your client. And approving projects, increasing funding, or implementing tax incentives are usually on the request list when legislators come to call.

1. First complete the Plan of Attack form for this project.

    It will help you determine the tone for the speech and structure the argument so that it is logical and interesting.

2. Write a 5 to 10- minute speech for your president/CEO.

    Read it aloud and mark any sections that are not easy to read. You will know when you run out of breath, stumble over a phrase, or start to bore yourself. Revise these sections so they sound like speech.

3. Identify and describe any graphics or visual support you will produce to support the speech.

4. Evaluate the speech.

Exercises, Chapter Twelve
When the News Isn't Good: Crisis Messages

■ Exercise 12-1: Crisis Planning

Refer to the background information "Crisis Writing" in your client profile. It describes a situation that may affect your client in a negative way, bringing negative publicity and possible long-term problems. It will affect your client's relationships with at least some of its publics. It calls for a communication response through the mass media as well as possible other strategies.

Storyboard Title:

Your first task is to develop a communications strategy that addresses the crisis situation. Prepare the strategy as a report to the Board of Directors. It should be based on your answers to the following questions.

- Why is this a crisis? What would happen if you did not make a communication response?

- Which if any of the audience(s) you identified in the "Getting Started" exercise will be affected by this situation? Are there any other audiences you should consider? How quickly must each of these audiences be reached?

- Which of the methods of reaching your publics (that you identified in the "Getting Started" exercise) would you recommend now? Why? Given that this is a crisis, should you consider other media as well?

- Generally, what message should each of the audiences receive? Who will be the best spokesperson for each audience? Why?

- Will more than one communication message or method be necessary? If so, what communications do you propose, and on what schedule?

- Will your client's legal counsel be involved in your proposed communication plan? Why or why not? What do you expect legal counsel to advise? What is your response to this advice?

■ Writing Assignment 12-2: News writing in a crisis

Also see Plan of Attack Forms

Organizations "leak" information frequently and quickly, especially when the news is bad. Accordingly, the news media have gotten wind of your client's crisis situation and they are calling you for a response. Even if your strategy was to communicate privately with a few audiences, it appears that you must make a public statement in the press.

1. Begin by completing the Plan of Attack form for this project.

   It will help you to understand the type of crisis you are dealing with and the public/s you must reach, and to identify the spokesperson/s and collateral materials that will help you respond to the crisis.

2. Write the media release that you will use to disseminate the "bad news" to the public(s) you want to reach through the mass media. Your instructor may allow you to execute another written strategy for reaching a public you need to reach if the mass media are not appropriate.

3. Define additional written and visual materials, if any, that you should have available as part of your response? When do you expect to need them? Which of these have you already written as part of this text?

4. Evaluate the release/ document..

■ Exercise 12-3: Crisis communications to special audiences

Refer to the public relations strategy for dealing with the crisis situation that you defined in exercise12-1. Which of your audiences is/are unlikely to be reached by the media release? Which ones will not be satisfied by it? Which ones do you need to communicate with simply to protect your client's relationship?

1.   Choose two of the publics. Write the message for each of these publics, indicating whether the communication is the script a representative will use on a personal call, the text of an individual or bulk fax, a memo, letter or a web page.

2.   Assume that you have newsletters due to be sent to both your internal and external publics within a week.

- Should you include articles about the crisis in these newsletters?

- Why or why not? Assuming that you decide yes, write the article you would include in each of them.

- Would you include the same articles if the newsletter were not out for another month? If so, how would they be different?

Chapter Thirteen

The Multi-purpose Medium: Writing for the Web

■   Exercise 13-1: Researching web statistics

Statistics on web use change almost daily and depend on the organization amassing the information and the methodology used.

1.   Conduct your own research to identify current statistics regarding who uses the Web and how it is used. Start by consulting the web sites used for the statistics in this chapter or that are listed as "References and resources" at the end of the chapter. Try to answer the following questions:

- How many businesses currently have web sites? How many in the US? How many small businesses?

- How many web users are there currently? How many are predicted ten years from now?

- How are public relations practitioners making use of the Web for their day-to-day operations? Pay particular attention to data for your Workbook client's sector.

- How could you get the data you found sent to you automatically without having to search for it regularly?

2.   One of the sources you should explore is the website of the PEW Internet and American Life project at www.pewinternet.org. What topics has this site reported on recently? What topics have they seen reason to update from previous reports? What topics would you suggest that they research? If this subject interests you, sign up for the free e-mail announcements about new surveys as they are released.

■   Exercise 13-2: Your publics and the Web

1.   Which (if any) of the publics you identified for your client in the "Getting Started" exercise do you expect could be effectively reached?

- Through a web site?

- By e-mail?

2. Why would you prefer the Internet to print or broadcast media as the medium by which to reach them? Why wouldn't you prefer the Internet?

3. For what specific purpose(s) would you use the Internet to reach each of these publics?

■ Exercise 13-3: Researching and assessing newsgroups

1. What newsgroups and mailing lists can you find for your client? As a starting point we suggest seeking groups that are interested in: pharmaceutical reform, poverty or homelessness, ISP regulations, or the future of higher education or the effect of distance learning technology on higher education.

2. What criteria will you use to determine whether to recommend these groups to your client?

3. Your web monitoring identifies a newsgroup that is discussing the following topic related to your client. Write a response to the newsgroup giving your client's position on the subject.

   - Central College ....Privacy of student records
   - CommunicAID (Homes for All)........Privacy of client financial records
   - HealthWay Pharmacies ....Privacy of medical records
   - ValleyLINK.......................................Internet privacy

4. What pages (if any) on your client's web site should be available that you could refer people to as a resource for more information on the topics listed in Questions 3 and 4?

■ Exercise 13-4: Web site content and links

On a very general basis, a web site might be considered an electronic fact sheet. The difference, of course, is that web sites by nature force you to consider multiple publics, how the information will be organized (and linked) to satisfy these multiple publics, and the amount of information you can include.

1. Identify several real-world competitors for your client. Review their web sites and list below the topics they include on the home page. If your client is a non-profit, you might consider as a competitor other organizations who would compete for the same funding.

   _____   _____   _____
   _____   _____   _____
   _____   _____   _____
   _____   _____   _____
   _____   _____   _____
   _____   _____   _____

2. List the topics you believe should be included in your client's web site. You may find it helpful to review your client's mission statement and goals when selecting these topics.

---

3. Identify several external sites your client should link to.

---

4. Now, using the topics you identified above, create a logic chart for your client's web site. You should be able to plan a minimum of 8-10 pages for the site. At least two of them should link to pages other than the home page. We have provided a basic plan similar to that used for the Childhood Asthma site, but we have left space for additional boxes. Or you may want to organize it differently.

    The top line will be the home page. The second line will include all topics you can access from the home page. One of the options should be an "About this organization," "About this web site," or "General Introduction" page (not necessarily using these titles) that will provide an overview for the casual visitor. Pages that derive from or link from these second-level pages will fall on lower lines. Refer to the text logic chart for the Childhood Asthma web site or the one for Project Bread on the text website (www.sagepub.org) as samples.

■ Writing Assignment 13-5: Web site copy

Also see Plan of Attack Form

In the previous exercises you have developed the basic content and flow of your client's web site. One of the sections was an introductory section, which will likely have hypertext links to other pages on the web site as well as possible links to external sites. It may have a title other than "Introduction" or "About this organization."

1. First complete the Plan of Attack form for this project.

    It will help ensure that you pay attention to the information needs and abilities of your multiple audiences.

2. Write the text for at least the introductory (level one) pages, keeping in mind the need for it to be concise, scannable, objective, credible and reflect your client's culture. Use bullet points and subheads to show the organization and highlight the important points. Your instructor may ask you to also write the copy for other pages.

Logic chart master for web site

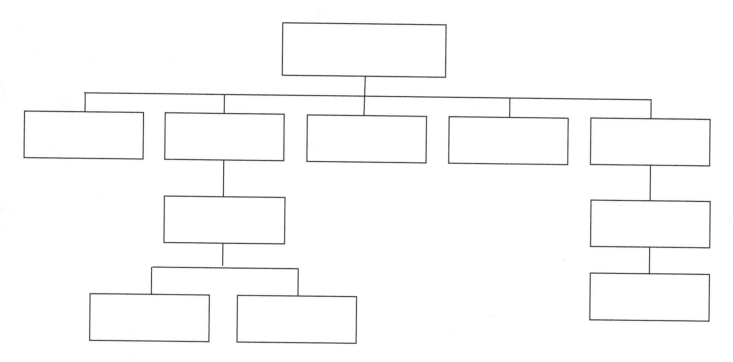

3.   Indicate hypertext links to other pages in your web site by underlining the appropriate text. Indicate and outline relevant external links (if any) with a "For more information" section at the end of the page.

4.   Review the text against your plan. Try to read it as if you were the various audiences at which it is aimed. Is it easily understood? Is it interesting enough to keep users at the site? Are links clear to previous pages? To further information? To the home page?

■ Exercise 13-6: On-line newsletters

1.   In Exercise 10-4 you determined the contents for a newsletter for one of your client's external publics. Some of the articles were also used for the employee newsletter; some were not.

Revisit the public newsletter and determine which of the articles would be appropriate for web letters posted on your web site and one sent by e-mail to a targeted mailing list.

Posted on web site   Targeted e-mail

_____

_____

_____

_____

_____

- If you eliminated any items from either list, why did you do so?
- What additional items should you include for either publication? Write them below.

2. How can you use the Web to establish a dialogue with the audience and to conduct research?

3. How will you present the web site newsletter? Will it be a button on the home page? Part of the "News" section? Will you post headlines or teasers on the home page?

4. Based on the contents you have defined above, how frequently do you expect to have to update the web letter contents?

5. How will the web articles differ from the articles you wrote for the printed newsletter? Will they be longer or shorter? Will you use any special presentation features such as bullet points or sub-heads? Will the style be more or less complex than with the printed text? What about the education level of your readership? Will it be higher or lower? How does this affect your copy?

6. Decide what the four most important articles for the web newsletter would be and write them. Remember what you know about writing for the Web when you do so.

■ Exercise 13-7: The Web in a crisis

In Exercises 12-1 through 12-3, you planned strategy and wrote messages to inform your client's publics about a situation that might be regarded as a crisis by some or all of them. This exercise will help you evaluate the Web as a possible medium for communication in this crisis.

1. Would the Web be an effective way to reach important publics with your crisis message? Why? Why not? Would you use it to replace or supplement other communications?

2. What public(s) could you expect to reach through the Web?

3. What web techniques will you use? web site? e-mail? newsgroups?

4. What external links, if any, will you recommend?

5. What tone will the web page have: e.g., factual, humorous, pro-active?

6. What visuals, if any, would you recommend?

■ Exercise 13-8: Web site design

In previous exercises in this chapter you have planned the contents and written some of your client's web site. You have also considered the need for navigational buttons to other pages and for links to external sites.

This exercise is to design the home page and at least two other pages for the web site including links to the other pages to give a sense of what is in the site.

- List any graphics you expect to use on any of the web site pages.
- What colors will you use on the web site? Remember, in Chapter 7 you identified colors that would identify your client. Are these suitable for the Web?
- Will you provide text-only options for any of the pages? If so, which ones?
- Will you provide any foreign language or other special handling for intercultural audiences?
- What would you do to maximize access to your web site for the handicapped?

Exercise 13-9: Promoting web sites

1. Decisions you make about key words will have an effect on how often your client's site is identified during web searches. To appreciate the importance of key words, conduct web searches using some of the following as key words. Try conducting the same search using at least two search engines. What are the first sites you get? Do the results differ? Why do they differ?

Key word	Search 1	Search 2	Search 3
AAA			
Numbers (1,2, etc.)			
Boomerang			
Abracadabra			
Your client's industry			
Your choice _____			

2. How will you inform relevant publics that your client now has a web site? Would this differ if your client was a large corporation or a government agency? How, for example, do you think the IRS tells the U.S. public that it has a web site?

3. The domain name you select and register will be part of your client's image on the Web. Given the immense number of web sites that are now registered, it is possible that your client's name has already been registered, especially for use on a regional basis.

     Identify five (5) possible domain names for your client, beginning with the client's name and including at least one that reflects the industry rather than the organization name. Remember the advantage (or disadvantage) of using extensions other than .com. As of the time of writing, you could test domain names to determine if they are already registered by conducting a search through the InterNIC web site: <www.internic.com>. You may also be able to do it through some of the other web sites listed under "Domain name registration and listing your URL" at the end of Chapter Thirteen. Which domain name will you recommend for your client? Why?

Exercise 13-10: On-line research

     Your client would like to take advantage of the opportunity to collect opinions and data about the visitors to the web site.

1. What information will you advise your client to collect? e.g., numbers, opinions on industry topics, demographics? Why?

2. Using the Childhood Asthma questionnaire shown in the text as a guideline, develop an online research questionnaire for your client. Consider especially what information your client would hope to obtain through a survey of visitors to its web site.

Persuasion for mass action: Advocacy campaigns, op-eds, and PSAs

■ Exercise 14-1: Endorsements and spokespersons

Celebrity endorsements and credibility . . . does one inevitably lead to the other or are we so inundated with famous spokespersons that we don't actually believe what they say?

1. Name as many celebrity endorsers as you can think of. What products do they endorse? Which, if any, influence your buying decisions (be honest).

2. Do you believe that the people you have identified actually use the products they endorse? Does it make a difference?

3. What three nationally known persons would you recommend as spokespersons to reach each of the following audiences?

Senior citizens:	_____
Teenagers:	_____
Gen-Xers:	_____
Young parents:	_____
Midwest farmers::	_____
Law enforcement officers:	_____
Bankers:	_____
New Yorkers:	_____
Californians:	_____
Texans:	_____

• What factors did you consider when making your selections?

• What celebrities would you recommend as spokespersons for a campaign for your client? First define an audience you want to reach and then nominate at least one celebrity with expertise in the industry and one whose charisma or name alone would appeal to the target audience. Do the same for two other publics.

Public	Spokesperson with expertise	Spokesperson with charisma
_____	_____	_____
_____	_____	_____
_____	_____	_____

■ Exercise 14-2: Understanding the opposite side

A key to writing effective persuasive copy is to understand the arguments that your competition or opponent will present. Refer to the background to Exercise 14-2 in your client profile for detail on a situation for which your client wants persuasive messages and answer the following questions.

1. How would you expect the publics you identified as important to your client to react to the situation facing your client?

2. Which of your client's publics could you turn to for support for your client's position? How can you reach these publics with the necessary message?

3. What publics would you expect would oppose your client's position?

   - Why would they do so?

   - What do they have to gain by doing so?

   - What arguments will they likely put forth against your position?

   - What arguments and evidence can you cite to refute their arguments?

■ Writing Assignment 14-3: Persuasive Letters: effective argumentation

Also see Plan of Attack Form

The background to "Persuasive messages" in your client profile describes a scenario in which your client might feel compelled to issue persuasive messages. The scenario affects two of the clients that hold opposing views on the subject. This scenario will be used for several exercises throughout this chapter.

First your client wants you to write a letter to the Anytown state legislative representatives urging them to support your client's position. You must provide the legislators with evidence that they can cite during legislative debates.

1. First complete the Plan of Attack form for this project.

   It will help you shape your argument and identify evidence that will resonate with the legislators.

2. Write a one-page letter that will persuade the legislators to support your client's position.

   What appeal will best make your point? You may invent or assume statistics that support your position.

3. Evaluate the letter.

   NOTE: As a public relations writer, you should know how to reach and address communications to government officials. Some generally accepted principles are:

   - Keep the letter brief – one page if possible.

   - Be factual. Support your position with information about how the legislation will affect you and others.

   - Ask for the legislator's support.

   - For federal legislators the suggested address style is:

The Honorable (full name)	The Honorable (full name)
United States Senate	United States House of Representatives
Washington, DC 20510	Washington, DC 20515
Dear Senator (last name only):	Dear Representative (last name only):

   We suggest you use a similar style for state legislators and other elected officials.

■ **Writing Assignment 14-4: Letter to the editor**

Also see Plan of Attack Form

Assume that the Anytown newspaper has printed an editorial on the issue described in the background to "Persuasion." The editorial came out in support of the organization with which your client is paired for this project. Your client wants you to write a letter to the editor of the paper presenting your client's position and seeking community support in persuading the legislature to vote as your client wants.

Remember, although a letter to the editor is technically to the person in the editorial chair, in fact the target audience is actually the readers who may have been swayed by the editorial.

1.   First complete the Plan of Attack form for this project.

It will help you focus your argument and choose and develop effective evidence.

2.   Write the letter.

Be certain to make clear both the issue and what you want the public to do as the result of your letter.

3.   Evaluate the letter.

NOTE: An especially good exercise is to also write the letter you believe your opposition would write. Then compare the two to ensure that you have effectively refuted or rebutted the opposition's argument even while promoting your own.

■ **Writing Assignment 14-5: Advocacy ads**

Also see Plan of Attack form

1.   Assume that the issues presented below are currently before Congress and that they affect both the general public and the workbook clients as designated.

- Central College. ....A bill to limit annual tuition increases for all institutions to the lesser of $300 or 10% of the previous year's tuition.

- CommunicAID. ....A bill to remove the tax-deductible status of charitable contributions by individuals.

- HealthWay Pharmacies ....A bill that requires pharmacies to provide children from families with incomes below the poverty line with medications at no cost and charge the state.

- ValleyLINK ....A bill to deregulate the industry to encourage greater competition and make it easier for small business to compete with large ones.

To determine whether your client should take a public stand or simply monitor the issue, look at the publics you identified in the "Getting Started" section. Complete the following chart to gauge whether your client needs to communicate publicly on the issue. Then answer the following questions.

Public	Is public a priority?	Is issue important to the public?

- Identify any other publics that are likely to be interested in the issue but which you have not identified as important to your client. Should they be important? If so, add them to the list of your client's publics.

- Taking one side of an issue is almost never a "win-win" situation. If your client takes such a position, which publics will you risk alienating? Are these publics important?

2. First complete the Plan of Attack form for this project.

3. Write the text and produce a rough design for the ad.

Given that each of the issues involves legislation before Congress, we suggest that the action each client seeks from a public advocacy ad is for readers to write their Congressional representatives asking them to support or reject the bill (depending on your client's position).

- Draft the headline, first paragraph and action line (what to do) of an advocacy ad that your client might run seeking this support. Remember, persuasion begins with making the issue relevant to the reader.

- Sketch or describe the graphic techniques you would use to attract readers' attention, e.g., photos, artwork, headline type/size, etc. Be specific.

4. Evaluate the ad to ensure that it will reach and resonate with the public/s you have identified as the target audience.

5. Identify two other controversial issues on which your client might also consider a public stance.

■ **Writing Assignment 14-6: Public Service Announcements**

Next month has been designated YourState Literacy Awareness Month, and the Anytown Literacy Council has obtained the agreement of a local TV station and the Anytown newspaper to run a series of public service announcements promoting the benefits of literacy.

Central College, CommunicAID, HealthWay Pharmacies and ValleyLINK Communications have each agreed to pay the production costs of a PSA as long as the PSA promotes a benefit of literacy that relates to the organization's industry and interests.

The Literacy Council has approved the following general topics for the four PSAs:

- Central College ....literacy for real life: e.g., driver's tests, employment tests
- CommunicAID..........literacy as a tool for combating poverty
- HealthWay ....literacy for understanding medical information
- ValleyLINK ....literacy for taking advantage of the Web

It is your job to create the PSA your client will provide to the Literacy Council. It may be a script and a storyboard for a 30-second TV spot or the copy and design for a full-page newspaper display ad. Special considerations with this project include exactly whom you will appeal to: i.e., those who are illiterate or those who know people who are illiterate. Why does this make a difference? You must also consider the relative merits of various media for reaching the publics you are targeting.

Remember that your ultimate aim is to promote literacy; your theme is the topic listed above. You may interpret the theme in any way you wish.

Public service announcements such as these provide an opportunity for public relations writers to write for audiences and on subjects that might not ordinarily be part of their jobs.

1. First complete the Plan of Attack form for this project.

2. Write three headlines for the ad.

   They should attract attention, introduce the theme, and be memorable.

3. Write the PSA, building to a concise final statement that gives your message.

   - If you are writing a broadcast PSA, refer to the guidelines for video/multi-media productions in Chapter Eleven for assistance.

   - If you are preparing a print ad provide: a headline, a description or mock-up of at least one graphic, two to three paragraphs of text and the final closing message.

     Remember, you are producing this message on behalf of the Literacy Council. Mention of your client is limited to a small visual-only "Paid for by ___" line at the end of the PSA.

4. Evaluate the PSA.

Exercises, Chapter Fifteen

Persuasion for individual action: Brochures, Proposals and Direct Mail

■ Exercise 15-1: Building effective mailing lists

Regardless of whether you are soliciting sales or donations, knowing whom to target is key to a campaign success. When direct mail is part of your public relations plan, this means having a good mailing list of people who are likely to respond positively, so the campaign is cost-effective.

1. Which of your client's publics could be reached effectively by a direct mail message? Consider factors such as whether there are enough members in that public to make a mailing cost-effective, whether you have available other means to reach them (e.g., newsletters), and whether you are seeking a specific behavioral response that warrants direct mail.

2. In question 1 above you identified possible publics for a direct mail campaign for your client. When purchasing a list from a list marketing company, you must provide the company with characteristics of the public you want to reach. List six demographic criteria that a list marketing company could use to identify a list for your client. Consider factors such as zip code, age, education, etc. Which are most important? Why?

■ __Writing Assignment 15-2:__ __Writing a direct mail appeal__

Also see Plan of Attack Form

One of the most common forms of direct mail is the fund raising appeal used by thousands of non-profit organizations each year to secure funding from their community supporters. It is a good exercise in identifying and developing an appeal that will resonate with a target audience. Just as the level of contributions of major donors and the general public will differ greatly, so too is the reason each will contribute and the appeal that will most effectively reach them.

- CommunicAID and ....Write a fund raising appeal for either your organization's
  Central College   Annual Fund* or for a specific, named purpose of your choice such as a scholarship or program fund.

- ValleyLINK and ....Write a fund raising appeal on behalf of the Literacy Council
  HealthWay Pharmacies   for which you produced a PSA. (See Exercise 14-5). You may write the appeal either for the Annual Fund* or for a specific, named project. The Literacy Council will be considered your client for this project.

- * NOTE: Unlike a fund for a specific purpose, an Annual Fund is conducted regularly for general purpose funding. It solicits relatively small contributions from a large number of donors. Direct mail and phonathons are the most common ways of conducting annual fundraising campaigns with large publics.

Your client has three aims with this letter: to solicit contributions, to generally promote the client's services, and to make the recipient feel a part of the "client family". Your client will insert a standard reply envelope and pledge card for the contributions.

1. First complete the Plan of Attack form for this project.

    It will help you explore and identify an appropriate appeal and develop the argument around that appeal.

2. Write a one- to two-page letter using any appeal you believe is appropriate for the audience. Be prepared to explain why you chose that appeal.

3. Create an envelope for the mailing.

    The standard envelope size for such a letter is a #10 envelope measuring 9 1/2" x 4 1/4". They will have addresses printed on the envelope and will be bar-coded for carrier route sorting.

    The envelope must take into account the message you developed in the letter and the restrictions on envelopes discussed in the text. Create a mock-up of the layout. Write the copy or artwork in approximately the size and colors (if appropriate) that you would use and in the position you would place it. Don't forget that return addresses are required for envelopes.

4. Evaluate the project.

■ Writing Assignment 15-3: Creating a brochure

Your course client wants a printed two- or three-color brochure that it can use in response to requests for information or as general information pieces at conferences and trade fairs.

You may create a brochure about your client itself or about one of its programs or affiliates. The flat (unfolded) brochure size will be 8 1/2" x 11" but it can be a portrait or landscape format.

1. First complete the Plan of Attack form for this project.

   It will help you select appropriate topics for the brochure and help ensure that the presentation is clear and easy to understand by your target publics.

2. Write all of the brochure text.

   Write it panel by panel beginning with the front cover. Indicate what goes on each panel (cover, first panel, flap, etc.)

3. Using page layout software or Word templates (if you have them) or creating a paste-up if you don't, create a mock-up of the finished brochure, indicating all colors, artwork and text. Fold the brochure as it would be folded.

4. Evaluate the brochure.

■ Exercise 15-4: Identifying grant and RFP sources

Research the Web to identify organizations for which your client might write a grant or respond to an RFP. Try government departments, industry organizations that relate to your client's industry and the Foundation Center (for non-profit organizations).

RFP source or grant agency

■ Exercise 15-5: Writing grants and proposals

When writing grant requests and proposals, your choice of words will be especially critical in the balancing act between objectivity and promotion. Following are typical requirements for audience-driven proposals, one from an RFP seeking commercial service providers and the other from a common grant application issued by a consortium of private foundations.

1. The following requirement is part of an RFP to be completed by:

   HealthWay Pharmacies — The RFP is seeking contractors to provide pharmaceutical services by mail to the members of the YourState Public Service Association (i.e., YourState government employees).

   ValleyLINK — The RFP is seeking contractors to provide ISP services for 20 school districts in East Valley, YourState.

   RFP requirement — "Describe your organization's experience in performing the service required under this contract."

2. The following requirement is part of a grant proposal to be completed by:

<u>CommunicAID</u> — which is applying for funding to support a summer family literacy program at the Elms Apartment complex.

<u>Central College</u> — which is applying for funding to extend its distance learning courses to institutions such as prisons, rest homes and military bases.

<u>Grant requirement</u> — "Describe your organization's current programs and activities."

Your task is to write two 3-paragraph responses for your client. The first should detail relevant facts only (you may invent additional facts relevant to this assignment). The second should be written persuasively enough to leave no doubt that your client is the most qualified respondent for the contract or grant.

Make sure that any statement you write can be supported or verified and remember that the responses should focus on your client's expertise as related to the proposed project. Choose specific examples to demonstrate relevant expertise.

Exercises, Chapter Sixteen

High Profile Projects: Annual Reports, Events and Expositions

The following exercises will take you through many sections of an annual report that a public relations writer might be responsible for. You will begin with an annual report to a public audience and then look at what would change if you were to produce the same report for an employee audience.

■ ## Exercise 16-1 Annual Report Planning

Look at the publics you identified in the "Getting Started" exercise as important to your client. List below all those that would be target publics for an external Annual Report (do not include employees). Next to each, determine which three of the listed annual report sections would be of most interest to that public. This will give you an indication of what will be most important in the annual report.

Audience/Public	Highlights	CEO message	Financial Information	Features.

Your next task will be to write the material for these four sections of the report.

■ Exercise 16-2: Writing highlights for interest and parallel structure

Whenever bullet point formats are used, they call attention to information that the reader expects will be important. On one hand, you therefore have an obligation to fulfill this expectation; on the other hand you can be quite sure that readers will at least begin to read anything in that format. That is why it is so effective for "highlights". If you choose them carefully, even readers who stop at that point will have read your most important messages.

1. Review your client's profile and the background information on the projects you have already completed and identify a list of highlights for the current year's annual report. The highlights should support a theme of success and supporting the community.

    You may assume that the financial information given in the profile will be the information reported in this report. Try to identify at least one financial highlight that supports or illustrates the theme.

2. Write the heading for the highlights.

    In column two rewrite the highlights into parallel structure so they follow logically from the heading.

■ Exercise 16-3: Writing the CEO message for Annual Reports

In Exercise 16-1 you identified publics for which the client would produce an annual report. These are the publics for which you wrote a feature story. You have also previously defined the interests and concerns of your client's publics. Review again what these publics want to know from and about your client.

1. What do you believe your target publics expect and/or want to know from your president/CEO in the annual report?

2. What themes do these concerns suggest for the CEO message? What topics should the CEO address . . . or avoid?

3. Write a one- to two-page message targeted to this public for your president or CEO's review. You should address all of the following:

    •   The organization's financial statements and/or growth statistics (included in the client profile).

    •   The year's activities. Information to consider for this section can be found in the background for the "News Writing," "Crisis," "Newsletter," and "Feature Writing" assignments.

    •   A legislative or industry issue that has affected your client, (e.g., privacy or Internet regulations or changes specific to the poverty, education, pharmaceutical or ISP industries).

    •   The outlook for the future. You may infer that it is positive.

■ Exercise 16-4: Annual report photos and captions

Features are often the occasion for including photos in an otherwise copy-filled annual report. Photos should be selected especially for their ability to tell a story and attract readers to the accompanying feature article.

Refer back to the feature you wrote in Exercise 10-2 and to the background information provided for that exercise. Briefly describe four photos you would like taken to illustrate the feature story. Write a caption for each photo that supports the theme of the story and the purpose of your client in using the feature.

Description of photo	Caption
_____	_____
_____	_____
_____	_____
_____	_____
_____	_____
_____	_____
_____	_____

Exercise 16-5: Interpreting numbers for charts and graphs

The value of charts and graphs in providing an "at-a-glance" picture of even complex results or trends cannot be overestimated. At the same time, neither can the potential for charts and graphs to mislead if they are not produced or read carefully. Refer to the charts and graphs section of Chapter Seven for a discussion and examples of effective charts and graphs.

The first step is to identify exactly what trends or numbers can and should be translated into graphic form. Look for changes or trends that are significant and that you want to point out to the reader.

Refer to the financial information and growth statistics provided in your client profile.

1. Create pie charts showing how your client earned and spent its money during the last year.

2. Create a bar chart that illustrates at least one of the growth statistics.

Exercise 16-6: Employee annual reports

You have already written the highlights, CEO message and feature article for an annual report to your client's external publics, but management also wants to prepare a report for employees. It can be either a hard copy, printed report or a report in video format. Review the documents for the public annual report and the interests and concerns that employees have about your client.

1. What is the purpose of the employee report? Does this differ from the purpose of the public report? If so, why?

2. You have the option to produce either a printed employee report or a video report. Given the theme of the public report, the location(s) of employees and their concerns, which would you recommend to your employer? Why?

3. Does the material you have already written address employee concerns? If not, what change in topics and/or approach do you recommend for each of the writing projects to suit the medium (print or video) you have chosen?

Recommendations for changes

Highlights _____

CEO Message _____

Feature _____

Financials _____

4.   If you have chosen a print report, write the text for the report using the contents defined above and create a simple layout. Draw boxes or simply sketch out and describe any photos or additional charts and graphs you need. If you have chosen a video report, write the script and produce a simple storyboard for the video. In either case you should remember that this report should focus on employees.

Exercise 16-7: Planning and writing for a special event

In previous exercises you have written documents related to the opening of a new office or center or to the start of a new project or program. You have announced this occasion in a pitch letter, and the media are ready to attend. This exercise will help you understand how these elements fit into what is necessarily a grand scale plan for hosting the grand opening or project launch function.

For an event to be a success, a number of planning, writing and research assignments need to happen on time and in a logical sequence. These include for example: invitations to guests, a pitch letter/invitation to local media, a speech for CEO, a speech for the guest speaker and media/information kits for media and invited guests as appropriate.

1.   Planning — With all of the elements to be put in place for the event, it will be wise for you to do some planning that is more formal than the planning you might do for individual documents.

- Two common tools of such planning are the Gantt and Pert charts. If your instructor chooses to discuss these tools, you may be able to prepare simple charts for this project

    - Create a Gantt chart to show the estimated start and finish dates of all the major activities you will be coordinating.

    - Create a PERT diagram to show the relationships between the events and the "hidden" events that you will be responsible for. For example, the CEO or president must approve copy, and you may need to get cost estimates on printing the invitations and ensure that the mailing list is checked and accurate.

- Alternatively you may create a simple planning checklist, including the documents to be completed, the people responsible and the dates by which each must be finished. For jobs that are your responsibility, break the projects into specific tasks (e.g., interviewing, first draft, graphics, etc.) to help you manage the parts.

2.   Guest list — Draft a guest list for this function (e.g., by organization, title or position, such as "Anytown mayor" or "Anytown city council"). Your client is planning to invite between 60 and 100 guests.

3.   Invitations — Write the text and design the invitation for this function. Take a look at the fonts available on your system to see how different fonts can influence the tone of your invitation. What font have you chosen? Why?

4. <u>Speeches</u> — Write two speeches for this event, one for your president/CEO and the other for a local legislator who has agreed to be guest speaker. Go back to the speechwriting assignment for help on this project. Read them again – preferably aloud – to ensure they are interesting, flow well and send your client's message. What visuals or other support material will you need for the speeches?

5. <u>Media relations</u> — Write a pitch letter to the local media to persuade them to attend and cover the function. Refer to Chapter Nine for assistance in writing the pitch letter. This has already been done.

6. <u>Media and information kits</u> —This event is an occasion for which you might use a media kit and/or an information/publicity kit. The following questions will help you determine the purpose and contents for the kit.

   - <u>Media kit</u> — You have invited the media to cover the event and at least one has indicated that a reporter will attend. What information should you provide to assist them? What special equipment or facilities are they likely to require?

     List the contents of the media kit. Be specific. Check those items you have already produced in a previous assignment.

   - <u>Information kit</u> — This provides considerable scope based on what you believe the audience will be interested in about the event and your employer. List the contents of the information kit; be specific. Check those items that you have already produced in a previous assignment.

   - What will you use to hold the kit? Will the folder you designed in Exercise 7-4 be suitable? If not, what changes would you make and why?

   - Assemble one of the kits, including documents you have previously produced and writing the text for any material you have not already produced.

Exercise 16-8: Exhibition communications

In the background to the "Trade Fairs and Conferences" in your client profile, we have provided information about a conference or industry trade fair that your client wants to attend, including exposition details, publicity opportunities and the service or program that your client wants to promote at the event. You may assume that your client has reserved a 10' x 10' exhibit space and that you have available a freestanding display unit for use as a background. The display unit is covered in a neutral color that coordinates with the organizational colors you selected in Exercise 7-3.

Prepare a plan for the exhibition for approval by your supervisor. Present the plan as a package with covering memo. It should answer the following questions and include the copy and design sketches for as many of the following elements as fit into your plan. We suggest you begin by reading through the entire assignment so you understand all of the options available and all of your employer's expectations for the exposition before you start planning.

1. Exhibition aims

   Why does your employer want to exhibit at this event? Which, if any, of your employer's publics do you expect will attend? What is your employer's aim regarding this public: e.g., sales, persuasion, solicitation of support, education, establish a new position, reinforce an existing one, differentiate your employer from the competition?

2.   Exhibition planning

  •   Develop a theme for your client's exhibit. The brochure you designed in Exercise 11-8 was developed for the same program that your employer is promoting at this exposition. You may be able to develop the brochure theme for the exhibit although you do not have to do so.

  •   Express this theme in a two-line slogan.

  •   Express this theme in a one-line slogan.

  •   What graphic expression(s) will you use to develop this theme? Think of the palm tree and the stress test used in the UAI examples in Chapter Sixteen.

  •   What activities, demonstrations, action, incentives, etc., will you use to attract visitors to the exhibit? Will you require additional exhibit space to accommodate this activity?

3.   Media coverage

Good public relations writers will examine every opportunity to obtain positive media coverage – in the mass media, trade press or exposition publications – for their clients

  •   Do your exhibit plans offer any opportunities to obtain media coverage for your employer? For example, is your employer introducing a new product or service? Will anything occur at your exhibit that will attract media attention, e.g., a celebrity appearance, an interesting demonstration or an original contest?

      Write a pitch letter that will persuade the local media to attend the exposition and write a feature on your employer's exhibit for their publication. What media will you send this pitch letter to?

  •   What about your own media, especially the newsletters and annual reports that you produce for your employer? What will you do at the exhibition to collect material for these publications?

4.   Pre-exhibition publicity

  •   Is a pre-conference mailer appropriate? If not, why not? To whom will you send it (if it is appropriate)?

  •   Is a pre-conference advertisement appropriate? If not, why not? In what media would you place it?

  •   Create either a one-sided mailer (3 3/4" x 8 1/2") or an advertisement (5 1/2" x 8 1/2") to promote your client's participation at the exhibition. You may assume that the reverse of the mailer is a mailing panel.

5.   Exhibition publicity

  •   Exhibition organizers have requested a one-paragraph description of each exhibitor that will be printed at no cost in the exhibition program. Consider whether the boilerplate paragraph you wrote in Exercise 8-3 is appropriate for this purpose. Does it support your client's aims at this exhibition? Is it appropriate for this audience? If so, you may submit it as part of the package. If not, make necessary changes before submitting it.

  •   Create an ad (size 5 1/2" x 4 1/4") for the exposition program.

6.	Exhibition research

In Exercises 11-2 and 11-4 you wrote letters to the editor and to your legislators about a public issue that is important to your client. The issue was described in Exercise 11-2. Your client now wants to use the exhibition to gather opinions on this subject and on the audience that attends the exhibition. Your IT Department has the capability to set up a computer program so that visitors can record their answers to multiple choice or yes/no questions simply by pressing buttons. You are limited to a total of six questions.

- Write the six questions, including the choices for any multiple-choice questions. You must gather data on the issue and the audience. Consider especially what your client wants to know about the visitors to the exhibit, e.g., age, sex, employment, health status, computer literacy, knowledge of legislation or educational interests. Review Chapter 5 and Appendix C for help in developing effective questions.

- How will you publicize the survey to obtain as many responses as possible?

7.	Exhibit

- Briefly describe and sketch the exhibit: What will you display? How will you carry out the theme? Will you recommend that the representatives wear, say or do anything special to carry out the theme?

- Write the text and sketch the design for the signs you will use on the backdrop. These can be text, charts or graphs or photos. You must use at least two signs. Indicate the position of the signs on your sketch.

8.	Exhibition collaterals

In Chapter 15 you wrote and designed a brochure for the program being promoted at this exhibition. Is this brochure appropriate for the exhibition? Why? Why not? What changes would you have made to the brochure if you had known of the exhibition before you created the brochure?

- Will you have any giveaways available at the exhibit? What do you want them to achieve?

- What give-away(s) will you recommend? Why? Consider audience demographics, numbers, exhibit theme, and relative cost (e.g., cheap/mass distribution, moderate cost/one-to-a-visitor limit, or expensive/limited quantity/select distribution.

- Workbook Figure 16.1 includes the actual spaces, called imprint areas, in which your message can be printed for five common giveaways. They were taken from actual gift catalogues to illustrate the range of shapes and sizes of the spaces you will typically have available for messages on giveaways.

	In practice, assume that you would recommend these as giveaways for your client. Write a message for each of the giveaways that will include all information you want printed on that item. Consider including logos, organization name, contact information, slogan and message, as appropriate.

9.	Evaluation

What criteria will you use to evaluate whether the exhibition was a success for your employer? How will you obtain the data for this evaluation? How will it influence your decisions about your employer's participation at the next exhibition?

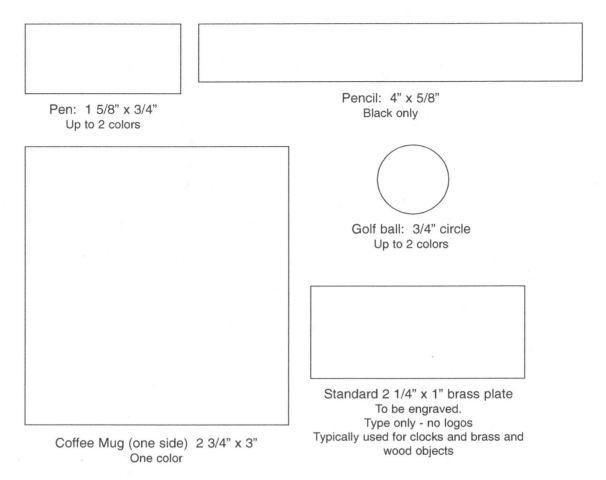

Pen: 1 5/8" x 3/4"
Up to 2 colors

Pencil: 4" x 5/8"
Black only

Golf ball: 3/4" circle
Up to 2 colors

Coffee Mug (one side) 2 3/4" x 3"
One color

Standard 2 1/4" x 1" brass plate
To be engraved.
Type only - no logos
Typically used for clocks and brass and
wood objects

Figure 16.1: Actuall size mock-ups of the space available for messages on a sampling of common give-aways. It is your task to write the text and design the layout for these give-aways.

What additional information, e.g., sales numbers, donations etc., will you look at long-term to determine the exhibition's success?

10.   Post-exhibition follow-up

- What contact will you make with the people who attended the exhibition and who left information for your mailing list?
- How will you capitalize on your employer's participation after the exhibition? Why?

Think of all the media we have discussed and how this exhibition could be included in any of them. Remember too, your employer's goals and determine if and how such publicity would fit into them.

Exercises in Editing

■ ## Editing Exercise 1: Précis-writing

Following is the first draft of a letter written by the project manager of a company that performs due diligence audits for banks (i.e., the company reviews accounts to determine if the bank did everything it was supposed to do on the accounts before they are audited).

Some of the comments that might be made about the letter are that it is "verbose," "repetitive," "confusing," and "self-serving." It would be hard to argue with a reader who simply wanted the writer to "get on with it." There seem to be four points that the writer is trying to make:

- OurCompany has done our job.
- YourCompany has not.
- YourCompany may be in trouble.
- OurCompany can help you out of trouble.

1. Your task is to make the letter shorter and clearer. Start by marking up the draft to eliminate unnecessary words and/or sentences. We have double-spaced the letter to make it easy for you to make your edits (just as it will be necessary for you to double- or triple-space media releases to make it easier for editors to do their jobs).

2. Rewrite the letter to improve and shorten the copy. Keep in mind the four points listed above as well as the need to use a style appropriate to the communication. Hint: it is a business letter carrying negative information to the president of the client company, but don't forget which points may be most important to the president of OurCompany . . . your boss.

Dear Sir:

This letter is to report on the audit I performed yesterday on the due diligence project that the audit team from OurCompany has undertaken on behalf of YourCompany. I am pleased to say that our audit team reports that OurCompany has met our contractual obligations for the project. Unfortunately, the audit also appears to show that YourCompany may have potential for violations under Section §XXX of the Federal Regulations with, of course, the accompanying liability. Please note that I cannot absolutely confirm that you will be potentially liable for these violations without additional information.

The violation stems from the fact that the information is incomplete on the accounts our audit team reviewed. It is possible that these discrepancies could have been identified earlier had YourCompany provided account update tapes at the weekly frequency agreed upon in our contract, however, to date OurCompany has received only one update, on July 24, this year, including the 754 accounts we were working as of July 15th. I specifically requested an update tape at my September 5th meeting with Susan VicePresident and Martin Director. Martin

Director acknowledged the request and Susan VicePresident committed to generating it. To date we have yet to receive the tape, updating either the original 754 accounts or the additional placements. It is essential that we receive it immediately.

If these violations exist, and I sincerely believe they do, the critical task is to address them as quickly as possible through a fix-it program that can be provided by OurCompany. Jonathan President or I will be happy to talk with you further about the problem and the fix-it solution. Please call either of us at 800-000 0000 if you have any questions or to discuss the issues we have raised. I look forward to working with you to resolve this situation.

Sincerely,

Editing Exercise 2: Copyediting

1. Use standard copyediting marks and manuscript notations to correct the errors in the letter shown as Exhibit E.2. A sales representative drafted it after visiting a prospective client. Be sure to consider spelling, punctuation, grammar and paragraphing in your review.

Joe Smith
~~drector~~ Director of Purchasing

ABC Industrys

123 Main Street Anywhere, US 00000

Dear ~~Ms. Smit~~ Mr. Smith:

I would like to take this opporutnity to extend my thanks to you for letting me meet with you the other day. I'm glad we had the opportunity to talk over lunch, to

I'll give you a call back in a week ~~or thereabouts~~ to ~~talke~~ talk about the propoosal I left with you. By that time you should have had a chance to look over it. If you have any questions about it before then, just give me a call at 1-800-542-5016. If I'm ~~nhot~~ not around, I'll call you ~~bak whne~~ back when I get a ~~change~~ chance. Thanks again.

Exhibit E.2: Copyediting a letter

2. While you're at it, the sales department wants you to review the mailing labels for the next client newsletter. Use standard copy editing marks to correct the errors. Pay special attention to unusual names and put a question mark next to any that should be re-checked by the sales representative. NOTE: These are actual, not fictitious, states.

Ms. Shelia Beck

Director of Financial Aid

Alabam State University

PO. Box 32

Forrest, TX 00000
AL

Robert CC. Woods

Director of Studnt Aid
student

Tennnesse Instutite

1015 42nd Street

Nashvile, TN 55555

Mr. Bryan Roberts

Finncial Aid Direction

Marshall College

663 Universty Drive
University or

Baton Rouge, LA 22222
FL

Mr. Chris Randolpf
Randolph

V President of Finance

University of Tempe

Tempee, AX 77777
Tempe, AZ

Plan of Attack Form: Letters of Application

Name: _____ **Date due:** _____

Client: _____

1. In your own words, what is this assignment?

2. From your client's point of view, what is the purpose of this assignment?

3. Who are the primary public/s for this document? What do you know about them that is relevant for this exercise? Why are they important? What attitude will they have about the message?

4. What medium/media will you use for this project? Why is the medium/media appropriate for this project? Why is it appropriate for reaching this public?

5. What do the audience, purpose and medium tell you about how you should write this document? Consider such factors as structure, language, style, etc. (Be specific)

6. What messages are you trying to send with this document? (List at least three.)

7. What *public relations message/s* will you send? How will you work them into the document?

8. **Strategy for letters of application:**

To help you determine the content that will most effectively match your skills with the organization's needs, complete the following chart. Look carefully at the ads. What skills are the organizations looking for? What personal attributes? Consider *relevant* coursework, employment, activities, and leadership and/or participation. Although you would likely include all of them in a résumé, you will highlight only the most important in a letter. Put asterisk next to the three most important ones. These will be the main points of your letter.

Organization's Needs	Your Abilities and Achievements	Evidence, e.g. projects, successes, testimonials

Self-evaluation:

1. Do you think this letter will succeed in getting you an interview?

2. What are the strengths of your letter?

3.. What are its weaknesses?

4.. How can you improve it?

Plan of Attack Form: Fact sheets, Boilerplates, Bios

Name: _____ **Date due:** _____

Client: _____

1. In your own words, what is this assignment?

2. From your client's point of view, what is the purpose of this assignment?

3. Who are the primary public/s for this document? What do you know about them that is relevant for this exercise? Why are they important? What attitude will they have about the message?

4. What medium/media will you use for this project? Why is the medium/media appropriate for this project? Why is it appropriate for reaching this public?

5. What do the audience, purpose and medium tell you about how you should write this document? Consider such factors as structure, language, style, etc. (Be specific)

6. What messages are you trying to send with this document? (List at least three.)

7. What *public relations message/s* will you send? How will you work them into the document?

8.　**Strategy for fact sheets, backgrounders and bios**

　　　　List the topics you want to cover in this document for this audience. What will the audience want to know about your client? What details will illustrate these topics best and make them interesting? Organize the fact sheet by numbering the items in the order in which you will present them. Consider which should be presented together. Which follow logically from another topic? Which are most/least important? This project can also be done for a bio as you define the information that will introduce the person on personal and professional levels.

_____

_____

_____

_____

_____

_____

_____

_____

_____

_____

9.　　　　What graphic elements and/or treatments can you use to make this fact sheet visually appealing?

Self-evaluation

1.　　　　Do you believe the fact sheet effectively introduces your client? Will people read it?

2.　　　　What are its strengths?

3.　　　　What are its weaknesses?

4.　　　　How can you improve it?

Plan of Attack: Press Releases

Name: _____ **Date due:** _____

Client: _____

1.   In your own words, what is this assignment?

2.   From your client's point of view, what is the purpose of this assignment?

3.   Who are the primary public/s for this document? What do you know about them that is relevant for this exercise? Why are they important? What attitude will they have about the message?

4.   What medium/media will you use for this project? Why is the medium/media appropriate for this project? Why is it appropriate for reaching this public?

5.   What do the audience, purpose and medium tell you about how you should write this document? Consider such factors as structure, language, style, etc. (Be specific)

6.   What messages are you trying to send with this document? (List at least three.)

7.   What *public relations message/s* will you send? How will you work them into the document?

8. **Strategy for press releases**

- Who will be the spokesperson/s for this release? Why?

- What is the news? What news determinant does it meet? What does this tell you about the lead sentence for the story?

- Why will the local press be interested in this news? What can you do in the story to ensure the press is interested?

In the following chart, briefly describe each paragraph.of the release, remembering to work in Inverted Pyramid format. Put an asterisk next to those paragraphs in which you expect to include a public relations message on behalf of your client.

1. _____
2. _____
3. _____
4. _____
5. _____
6. _____
7. _____

Self-evaluation

1. Do you believe the media will run this release? Why/why not?

2. What are its strengths?

3. What are its weaknesses?

4. How can you improve it?

Plan of Attack: Pitch Letters

Name: _____ **Date due:** _____

Client: _____

1.   In your own words, what is this assignment?

2.   From your client's point of view, what is the purpose of this assignment?

3.   Who are the primary public/s for this document? What do you know about them that is relevant for this exercise? Why are they important? What attitude will they have about the message?

4.   What medium/media will you use for this project? Why is the medium/media appropriate for this project? Why is it appropriate for reaching this public?

5.   What do the audience, purpose and medium tell you about how you should write this document? Consider such factors as structure, language, style, etc. (Be specific)

6.   What messages are you trying to send with this document? (List at least three.)

7.   What *public relations message/s* will you send? How will you work them into the document?

8. **Strategy for Pitch Letters**

Generally you would not send a pitch letter to all media in your area unless you can provide each one with a unique story angle and/or exclusive access to a celebrity or photo opportunity. News editors may be reluctant to commit their staff to what they may consider a feature rather than news story if they have to compete with other media outlets for special coverage.

Instead, adopting an approach targeted at indiidual media will likely be more successful.

• Identify three (3) specific media outlets (or news beats) that you would like to interest in the story. For each of these media, identify a unique story interest, curiosity factor or appeal to readers, viewers or listeners? Consider whether the story might have an angle that would interest business, or science or lifestyle or other special reporters or publications, for example.

Medium/special reporter   Unique story interest for that medium

_____   _____

_____   _____

_____   _____

What audio, video of photo opportunity would you make available to each of these media?

Medium/special reporter   Photo/video/audio opportunity

_____   _____

_____   _____

_____   _____

Which of the above three media is most likely to run the story? Why?

Identify the basic information that must be included in the pitch letter.

• What is happening?_____

• Who will be involved? _____

• When will the event take place?_____

• Where will the event take place? _____

Self-Evaluation

1. What are the strengths of the pitch letter?

2. What are its weaknesses?

3. How can you improve it?

Plan of Attack: Feature Writing

Name: _____ **Date due:** _____

Client: _____

1.   In your own words, what is this assignment?

2.   From your client's point of view, what is the purpose of this assignment?

3.   Who are the primary public/s for this document? What do you know about them that is relevant for this exercise? Why are they important? What attitude will they have about the message?

4.   What medium/media will you use for this project?   Why is the medium/media appropriate for this project? Why is it appropriate for reaching this public?

5.   What do the audience, purpose and medium tell you about how you should write this document? Consider such factors as structure, language, style, etc.   (Be specific)

6.   What messages are you trying to send with this document?   (List at least three.)

7.   What *public relations message/s* will you send?   How will you work them into the document?

8. **Strategy for feature writing**

You should be able to identify at least four topics for a human interest feature story based on the information provided in the assignment background. List them below. What approaches and techniques discussed in this section would be appropriate to attract and hold the readers' attention for the topic you have chosen for the story? Circle the approach you will use.

Topic/Description	Approach/Technique

In the chart below, plot out how you will develop one of the topics listed above into a feature story using one of the approaches you have identified. Use as many lines as necessary to briefly describe the sections of the story.

1. _____

2. _____

3. _____

4. _____

5. _____

6. _____

7. _____

8. _____

9. What photos and/or graphics do you suggest to support the story?

Self-evaluation

1. What are the strengths of your feature story? What are its weaknesses?

2. How can you improve it?

Plan of Attack: Writing news for newsletters

Name: _____ **Date due:** _____

Client: _____

1. In your own words, what is this assignment?

2. From your client's point of view, what is the purpose of this assignment?

3. Who are the primary public/s for this document? What do you know about them that is relevant for this exercise? Why are they important? What attitude will they have about the message?

4. What medium/media will you use for this project?   Why is the medium/media appropriate for this project? Why is it appropriate for reaching this public?

5. What do the audience, purpose and medium tell you about how you should write this document? Consider such factors as structure, language, style, etc. (Be specific)

6. What messages are you trying to send with this document?   (List at least three.)

7. What *public relations message/s* will you send?   How will you work them into the document?

8. **Strategy for "news" articles for newsletters**

- Who will be the spokesperson/s for this article? Why? If different from the spokesperson in the media release, why?

- What is the news? What news determinant does it meet? What does this tell you about the lead sentence for the story? Would a feature lead be appropriate? If so, what?

- How will this article differ from the media release? For example, what might you include that you did not include in the media release?

In the following chart, briefly describe the structure of the article. Put an asterisk next to those paragraphs where you expect to include the public relations message.

1. _____
2. _____
3. _____
4. _____
5. _____
6. _____
7. _____

- What photos and/or graphics would you suggest to accompany the story?

Self-evaluation

1. What are the strengths of the article?

3. What are its weaknesses?

4. How can you improve it?

Plan of Attack: Scriptwriting

Name: _____ **Date due:** _____

Client: _____

1.   In your own words, what is this assignment?

2.   From your client's point of view, what is the purpose of this assignment?

3.   Who are the primary public/s for this document? What do you know about them that is relevant for this exercise? Why are they important? What attitude will they have about the message?

4.   What medium/media will you use for this project?   Why is the medium/media appropriate for this project? Why is it appropriate for reaching this public?

5.   What do the audience, purpose and medium tell you about how you should write this document? Consider such factors as structure, language, style, etc.   (Be specific)

6.   What messages are you trying to send with this document?   (List at least three.)

7.   What *public relations message/s* will you send?   How will you work them into the document?

8.   Strategy for scriptwriting

   1.   Remember the options we discussed regarding themes, approaches, evidence and appeals
          for feature articles. They work equally well for video scripts. Identify four approaches
          you could use to develop the theme for your client's video. Put an asterisk next to the
          one you will use.

          *   _____

          *.   _____

          *   _____

          *   _____

   2,   Who will you use as "voices" to speak on the video? Who will narrate it to provide con-
          tinuity? Who will speak on specific topics, perhaps being interviewed or use as guides?
          These voices may or may not be the same. Do not forget the potential for using "profes-
          sional voices" but consider carefully what voices can be professional and what ones
          must be actual members of your client's staff. How many voices are appropriate for
          seven minutes?

          Voice   Topic

          _____   _____

          ._____   _____

          _____   _____

          _____   _____

          Why have you chosen each of these voices?

   3.   Briefly describe the graphics you will use. Will they be line art/drawings, cartoons, live
          footage of staff and/or clients, headings and title slides, etc. Why will you use these
          graphics rather than other possibilities?

Self-evaluation

1.   What are the strengths of the script?

3.   What are its weaknesses?

Plan of Attack: Writing news for broadcast

Name: _____ **Date due:** _____

Client: _____

1.   In your own words, what is this assignment?

2.   From your client's point of view, what is the purpose of this assignment?

3.   Who are the primary public/s for this document? What do you know about them that is relevant for this exercise? Why are they important? What attitude will they have about the message?

4.   What medium/media will you use for this project?   Why is the medium/media appropriate for this project? Why is it appropriate for reaching this public?

5.   What do the audience, purpose and medium tell you about how you should write this document? Consider such factors as structure, language, style, etc.   (Be specific)

6.   What messages are you trying to send with this document?   (List at least three.)

7.   What *public relations message/s* will you send?   How will you work them into the document?

8. **Strategy for writing news for broadcast**

- Read aloud the press release you wrote in Exercise 9-4, noting places that are not easy to read or to pronounce. If you stumble when reading it, you can be certain it will be even more difficult for someone who does not know the story. These sections need to be rewritten.

- It is likely that your press release will be longer than 1 minute. Identify information that you can do without. You should be able to "cut from the bottom" in the same way a press editor would do.

- Identify the names of places and people that need pronunciation guides. Write the pronunciation guide.

Press Release copy   Rewritten for broadcast

_____   _____
_____   _____
_____   _____
_____   _____
_____   _____

- Identify numbers that require simplifying and/or spelling out for easy reading? Don't forget the need to write out "dollars" rather than use dollar signs.

Press release copy   Rewritten for broadcast

_____   _____
_____   _____
_____   _____
_____   _____

- Assume that you will provide either an actuality or an A- or B- roll with the release. Write the instructions for this material.

Self-evaluation

1.. What are the strengths of the broadcast release?

2. What are its weaknesses?

Plan of Attack: Speechwriting

Name: _____ **Date due:** _____

Client: _____

1. In your own words, what is this assignment?

2. From your client's point of view, what is the purpose of this assignment?

3. Who are the primary public/s for this document? What do you know about them that is relevant for this exercise? Why are they important? What attitude will they have about the message?

4. What medium/media will you use for this project? Why is the medium/media appropriate for this project? Why is it appropriate for reaching this public?

5. What do the audience, purpose and medium tell you about how you should write this document? Consider such factors as structure, language, style, etc. (Be specific)

6. What messages are you trying to send with this document? (List at least three.)

7. What *public relations message/s* will you send? How will you work them into the document?

8.   **Strategy for speechwriting**

- Which of the structures described in the text for feature writing and/or speechwriting will you use to develop your argument? Why?

- What tone is appropriate for this speech? e.g., formal, casual, funny, overtly persuasive, laudatory? etc. Why? How will this affect your writing?

Completing the following chart will help you identify points you want to make and the evidence you have to support them. Three main points are ample for a 10-minute speech, so select carefully. It will also give you a structure for the speech. Remember that you have two aims for this speech: introducing your client and pleading a case of your choice.

Section	Description/Main Points	Examples/arguments
Introduction		
Body		
Conclusion		

- What response (if any) do you want from the audience? What call to action will you use?

- What visual aids will you make available to support the speech? What handouts? Why?

<u>Plan of Attack:</u> Crisis Writing

Name: _____ **Date due:** _____

Client: _____

1. In your own words, what is this assignment?

2. From your client's point of view, what is the purpose of this assignment?

3. Who are the primary public/s for this document? What do you know about them that is relevant for this exercise? Why are they important? What attitude will they have about the message?

4. What medium/media will you use for this project? Why is the medium/media appropriate for this project? Why is it appropriate for reaching this public?

5. What do the audience, purpose and medium tell you about how you should write this document? Consider such factors as structure, language, style, etc. (Be specific)

6. What messages are you trying to send with this document? (List at least three.)

7. What *public relations message/s* will you send? How will you work them into the document?

8.   **Strategy for crisis writing**

1.   Is this a crisis for your client? Why or why not?   What type of crisis is it, (e.g., natural disaster, legal, human error, etc.)?What damage/consequences could your client suffer as the result of this situation?

2.   What public/s will be most affected by this crisis? Who will be the most credible spokesperson with this public? Why is this person credible?

3.   What other sources are likely to speak out on this topic? What are they likely to say? Are you compelled to respond to them or can you ignore them? Why?   What, generally, will be your crisis strategy (high profile, low profile; pro-active, reactive; internal-focus, external focus)?

4.   How quickly must you respond to the situation? Why?

5.   What ethical responsibilities do you have in this situation? To your public? To the media? To your client?

6.   What collateral support materials, if any, do you want to provide the media or other audiences?

Self-evaluation

1..   What are the strengths of thebroadcast release?

2.   What are its weaknesses?

3..   How can you improve it?

Plan of Attack: Writing for the Web

Name: _____ Date due: _____

Client: _____

1. In your own words, what is this assignment?

2. From your client's point of view, what is the purpose of this assignment?

3. Who are the primary public/s for this document? What do you know about them that is relevant for this exercise? Why are they important? What attitude will they have about the message?

4. What medium/media will you use for this project? Why is the medium/media appropriate for this project? Why is it appropriate for reaching this public?

5. What do the audience, purpose and medium tell you about how you should write this document? Consider such factors as structure, language, style, etc. (Be specific)

6. What messages are you trying to send with this document? (List at least three.)

7. What *public relations message/s* will you send? How will you work them into the document?

8. **Strategy for web site writing**

Refer to the logic chart and the pages you have defined for your web site, and begin to define the contents of specific pages. On the following chart, for each page list the page topic, the two or three points (maximum) you will present on that page, any graphics, (charts, photos, video links) you would like to include on the page, and any links to other sources.

- What opportunities can you provide for inter-activity? What opportunities will you provide, if any, for your client to gather information or feedback?

Page Description	Target Audience	Points to Cover	Graphic, audio, video elements	Desired Links

Self-Evaluation

1. Have you addressed the needs of all of your target publics? How would you resolve this?

2. What is the primary strength of your web site?

3. What is the primary weakness of your web site?

Plan of Attack: Persuasive Letters

Name: _____ **Date due:** _____

Client: _____

1.	In your own words, what is this assignment?

2.	From your client's point of view, what is the purpose of this assignment?

3.	Who are the primary public/s for this document? What do you know about them that is relevant for this exercise? Why are they important? What attitude will they have about the message?

4.	What medium/media will you use for this project? Why is the medium/media appropriate for this project? Why is it appropriate for reaching this public?

5.	What do the audience, purpose and medium tell you about how you should write this document? Consider such factors as structure, language, style, etc. (Be specific)

6.	What messages are you trying to send with this document? (List at least three.)

7.	What *public relations message/s* will you send? How will you work them into the document?

8. **Strategy for letters to legislators and other persuasive letters**

- Who should sign the letter? Why? What credibility does your organization and the signer have? How can you make this credibility clear?

- Why might the legislator support (or not support) your position? This will help you identify points to raise and arguments to rebut.

In the following chart define the three main points you want to make. Then define two statistics, facts or pieces of evidence to support each point. Remember, part of your aim is to provide evidence the legislator can use when presenting your argument. Also define what you expect will be the primary opposing argument and two ways you can refute it.

Point or argument	Evidence
1.	1. 2.
2.	1. 2.
3.	1. 2.
Opposing:	1. 2.

- What do you want the legislator to do as the result of your letter?

- What graphics or information (if any) could you also provide to support your argument?

Self-evaluation

1. What are the strengths of your letter?

3. What are its weaknesses?

Plan of Attack: Letters to the Editor

Name: _____ **Date due:** _____

Client: _____

1. In your own words, what is this assignment?

2. From your client's point of view, what is the purpose of this assignment?

3. Who are the primary public/s for this document? What do you know about them that is relevant for this exercise? Why are they important? What attitude will they have about the message?

4. What medium/media will you use for this project? Why is the medium/media appropriate for this project? Why is it appropriate for reaching this public?

5. What do the audience, purpose and medium tell you about how you should write this document? Consider such factors as structure, language, style, etc. (Be specific)

6. What messages are you trying to send with this document? (List at least three.)

7. What *public relations message/s* will you send? How will you work them into the document?

8.   **Strategy for letters to the editor**

- Who should sign the letter? Why? What credibility does your organization and the signer have? How can you make this credibility clear?

In the following chart define the two or three main points you want to make. Then define two statistics, facts or pieces of evidence to support each point. Remember the benefit of finding appeals that the public can relate to. Also define what you expect will be the primary opposing argument and two ways you can refute it.

Point or argument	Evidence
1.	1. 2.
2.	1. 2.
3.	1. 2.
Opposing:	1. 2.

- What do you want the reader to do as the result of your letter? Remember, you are looking for support. With whom? What can the reader do?

Self-evaluation

1.   What are the strengths of your letter?

2..   What are its weaknesses?

Plan of Attack: PSAs

Name: _____   **Date due:** _____

Client: _____

1.   In your own words, what is this assignment?

2.   From your client's point of view, what is the purpose of this assignment?

3.   Who are the primary public/s for this document? What do you know about them that is relevant for this exercise? Why are they important? What attitude will they have about the message?

4.   What medium/media will you use for this project? Why is the medium/media appropriate for this project? Why is it appropriate for reaching this public?

5.   What do the audience, purpose and medium tell you about how you should write this document? Consider such factors as structure, language, style, etc. (Be specific)

6.   What messages are you trying to send with this document? (List at least three.)

7.   What *public relations message/s* will you send? How will you work them into the document?

8. **Strategy for Public Service Advertisements**

1. How does the issue of literacy benefit the public you have chosen to target? How will literacy benefit them? Why are they interested in the subject?

2. What is the message to this public? What do you want them to remember? to do?

3. What will make this message relevant to the public you have chosen? This is your theme or "hook." Consider the lifestyles, values, goals, and interests of the target public. How will you develop this theme?

4. In one sentence or less, write your primary message.

5. Refine the primary message into an attention-getting headline or slogan.

6. What scenario, visuals will support this message?

Self-evaluation

1. What are the strengths of your PSA?

3. What are its weaknesses?

4. How can you improve it?

Plan of Attack: Advocacy Ads

Name: _____   **Date due:** _____

Client: _____

1.   In your own words, what is this assignment?

2.   From your client's point of view, what is the purpose of this assignment?

3.   Who are the primary public/s for this document? What do you know about them that is relevant for this exercise? Why are they important? What attitude will they have about the message?

4.   What medium/media will you use for this project? Why is the medium/media appropriate for this project? Why is it appropriate for reaching this public?

5.   What do the audience, purpose and medium tell you about how you should write this document? Consider such factors as structure, language, style, etc. (Be specific)

6.   What messages are you trying to send with this document? (List at least three.)

7.   What *public relations message/s* will you send? How will you work them into the document?

8.   **Strategy for advocacy ads**

- Identify the issue your client is facing. What do you want the target public to do?

- What evidence will support your argument?

- What evidence will contradict your argument? How will you deal with it?

- What appeals will best sell your argument (e.g., sex, fear, peer approval, fact, emotion)? Why are the appeals appropriate to your target public.

- Identify your basic copywriting strategy (e.g., long/short; one-sided/two-sided; fact/emotion)? Why is this appropriate to the topic? To the target public?

- What graphic elements, if any, will you use to support or draw attention to your case?

Self-evaluation

1.   What are the strengths of the ad?

2..   What are its weaknesses?

3.   How can you improve it?

Plan of Attack: Direct Mail

Name: _____ **Date due:** _____

Client: _____

1.   In your own words, what is this assignment?

2.   From your client's point of view, what is the purpose of this assignment?

3.   Who are the primary public/s for this document? What do you know about them that is relevant for this exercise? Why are they important? What attitude will they have about the message?

4.   What medium/media will you use for this project? Why is the medium/media appropriate for this project? Why is it appropriate for reaching this public?

5.   What do the audience, purpose and medium tell you about how you should write this document? Consider such factors as structure, language, style, etc. (Be specific)

6.   What messages are you trying to send with this document? (List at least three.)

7.   What *public relations message/s* will you send? How will you work them into the document?

8. **Strategy for direct mail letters**

- Who will sign the letter? Why? How will you make this person's credibility clear?

In the chart below identify two appeals that you might use to attract attention and carry a theme in your letter to the target public Next to each, describe why this appeal would be appropriate for the target public, how you will attract the audience's attention, and what two facts or examples you will use to support the appeal.

	Appeal	Why is it appropriate?	Attract Attention/Evidence
1.			Attention: 1. 2.
2.			Attention: 1. 2.

- What do you want the target public to do as a result of your message?

- What other information might you include with the letter, if any? Why?

Self-evaluation

1. What are the strengths of your letter?

3. What are its weaknesses?

4. How can you improve it?

Plan of Attack: Brochures

Name: _____   **Date due:** _____

Client: _____

1. In your own words, what is this assignment?

2. From your client's point of view, what is the purpose of this assignment?

3. Who are the primary public/s for this document? What do you know about them that is relevant for this exercise? Why are they important? What attitude will they have about the message?

4. What medium/media will you use for this project? Why is the medium/media appropriate for this project? Why is it appropriate for reaching this public?

5. What do the audience, purpose and medium tell you about how you should write this document? Consider such factors as structure, language, style, etc. Be specific.

6. What messages are you trying to send with this document? List at least three.

7. What *public relations message/s* will you send? How will you work them into the document?

8. Strategy for brochures

- What theme will you use as the basis for this brochure? It should attract attention and convey or lead to the key message.

To develop the content for the brochure, complete the following chart, first listing seven possible topics or sections you want to include. We have already listed on for you. Briefly describe the section contents and why you would include it. This will help you identify the relative importance of the topics.. Finally determine the panel (front, inside 1, 2, or 3, flap, or back) each will go on. It is likely that you will not use all seven topics.

Section Topics	Describe contents and your aims for each	Panel
Contact Information		

- What photos/graphics and type techniques do you intend to use? For the cover? Inside?

Self-evaluation

1. What are the strengths of your brochure?

2.. What are its weaknesses?

3. How can you improve it?

Plan of Attack: _____

Name: _____ **Date due:** _____

Assignment: _____ **Client:** _____

1.   In your own words, what is this assignment?

2.   From your client's point of view, what is the purpose of this assignment?

3.   Who are the primary public/s for this document? What do you know about them that is relevant for this exercise? Why are they important? What attitude will they have about the message?

4.   What medium/media will you use for this project?   Why is the medium/media appropriate for this project? Why is it appropriate for reaching this public?

5.   What do the audience, purpose and medium tell you about how you should write this document? Consider such factors as structure, language, style, etc.   (Be specific)

6.   What messages are you trying to send with this document?   (List at least three.)

7.   What *public relations message/s* will you send?   How will you work them into the document?

8.   Strategy for writing _____

CPSIA information can be obtained
at www.ICGtesting.com
Printed in the USA
FSHW021714090119
54917FS